THE REFERENCE SHELF   VOLUME 46 NUMBER 2

AMERICA'S
CHANGING POPULATION

EDITED BY

OLIVER BELL

THE H. W. WILSON COMPANY

NEW YORK   1974

THE REFERENCE SHELF

The books in this series contain reprints of articles, excerpts from books, and addresses on current issues and social trends in the United States and other countries. There are six separately bound numbers in each volume, all of which are generally published in the same calendar year. One number is a collection of recent speeches; each of the others is devoted to a single subject and gives background information and discussion from various points of view, concluding with a comprehensive bibliography. Books in the series may be purchased individually or on subscription.

Library of Congress Cataloging in Publication Data

Bell, Oliver, comp.
    America's changing population.

    (The Reference shelf, v. 46, no. 2)
    SUMMARY: A compilation of newspaper and magazine articles about the American population, considering such topics as the significance of a declining birthrate and the feasibility of a population policy.
    Articles, reprinted from various periodicals.
    Bibliography: p.
    1. United States--Population--Addresses, essays, lectures. [1. Population] I. Title. II. Series.
HB3505.B4   301.32'9'73   74-8761
ISBN 0-8242-0522-7

—

PREFACE

In 1790 when the United States took its first census, 3,929,214 people were counted. The nation's numbers increased to an estimated 211.7 million at the beginning of 1974—a phenomenal jump in 184 years. Though we are not growing at as fast a rate as in the past, in the year 1973 an estimated 1.5 million persons were added to our numbers—more than one third of the entire US population when the nation began.

In the beginning the inhabitants of our country were hungry for people to settle the land. Probably no one questioned the need for more Americans. Now, however, we find ourselves in a different situation: though many see economic advantages in a rising population, others feel that we are overcrowded and depleting our resources. The latter group wishes to slow or halt our increase in numbers.

Estimates of future population are unreliable. For example, the National Resources Planning Board forecast in 1943 a US population of 156.549 million in 1970—a shortfall of about 50 million. Again, in 1947, the United States Census Bureau forecast only 163.312 million by the end of the twentieth century—but by 1960 the population had reached 180 million. After such failures, demographers became more cautious. In 1970, for example, the Census Bureau merely stated that, given various assumptions about births, deaths, and net immigration, the US population in the year 2000 would be between 250.286 million and 320.78 million, depending largely on the birthrate.

The prospect, then, is that our numbers will increase, but we don't know by how many. We do not know what leads women to choose to bear children nor why a woman chooses to bear more than two children. Indeed, the official

Commission on Population Growth and the American Future, when it reported in 1972, called for new funds to be appropriated to enable social scientists to investigate these and related questions.

We do know, however, that at present women are having fewer babies than formerly. If this trend continues, eventually the population will cease to increase. It is increasing now because there are so many women of childbearing age that at the present rate of a little over two children per woman the number of children born will keep the population growing for several decades. However, if immigration continues at its present rate (about 400,000 a year), the date for reaching a stationary population will be pushed further into the future.

Another issue is the changing composition of our population. Alterations in the way we live have resulted in empty classrooms in the lower grades and an increased proportion of individuals with college training, in suburbs housing more Americans than the central cities, and in improvements in the economic position of women and blacks. Furthermore, if the decline in the birthrate continues, the median age of the population will rise.

Is population increase good for the nation? Or, would we be better off with a stationary population? Or, perhaps with a smaller one? The answers to these questions vary with the respondent. The Population Commission in its 1972 report accepted continued growth but advocated a two-child family as the norm rather than a three-child one, thus favoring "moderate" growth. The goods and services needed for the additional citizens that a two-child norm would require could be provided, the Commission held, without seriously disrupting our economy and environment. In addition, the Commission felt that other problems inherent in growth, such as the increasing crowding of recreational facilities, would not become too pressing.

There are those who feel that the present population of the United States, given its current and probable future standard of living, is overtaxing the environment and will overtax it to a progressively greater degree. For instance, Zero Population Growth is an organization which calls for a halt to population growth by 1990. ZPG believes that the US environment is being abused and degraded and that it is in the national interest for us to reduce this burden by reducing our population.

The overriding issue, then, is this: Are we too few or too many? On this question honest differences of opinion exist. Scientists studying man in his environment are not yet sufficiently masters of their discipline to give us unequivocal answers.

What, if anything, needs to be done? On this there is no consensus. Some feel that the American people and their Government are slowly groping their way to a population policy and put their faith in a decline in the fertility of American women, without knowing whether a low level can be maintained. At the other extreme are those who call for a drastic cut in fertility, as does Zero Population Growth.

Meanwhile, the Federal Government is doing little about population—not much more than financing some birth-control clinics for the poor. Propaganda for fewer births is financed mainly by private groups, such as Planned Parenthood. Furthermore, there is strong opposition to legalized abortion: its opponents are driving toward a constitutional amendment forbidding it.

From a wider perspective, it seems certain that we will have to stop population growth at some point. At present rates of increase it will not be too many decades before the carrying capacity of the earth is reached. Then, population growth will have to stop. What is not certain is whether we will, calmly and intelligently, face the facts about population increase, work out a policy, and implement that policy.

This book takes the reader through a consideration of how fast we are growing to an analysis of the declining growth rate, to comments on the feasibility of a population policy in the light of current controversies over questions

of morality and discrimination, and finally to a consideration of the social and economic problems inherent in any
policy.

The editor wishes to thank the publishers and authors
who have granted permission to reprint selections in this
compilation.

OLIVER BELL

April 1974

A NOTE TO THE READER

The reader's attention is directed to two earlier Reference Shelf compilations dealing with topics with which
population growth is closely linked: *Protecting Our Environment* (Volume 42, Number 1), edited by Grant S. Mc-
Clellan, published in 1970; and *Priorities for Survival* (Volume 44, Number 6), edited by William P. Lineberry, published in 1973.

CONTENTS

I.   HOW FAST ARE WE GROWING?

EDITOR'S INTRODUCTION

Demography is largely a matter of numbers, a statistical science dealing with the number of persons living in given areas and the rate of growth or decline. In this opening section, the first article, by Trevor Armbrister, drawn from the *Reader's Digest,* presents some salient facts and trends revealed by the 1970 census about the citizens of the United States. Surprisingly, US population was shown to be increasing at a slower rate than previously. Moreover, many of the standards by which one can measure well-being showed a rise. The next selection, from the New York *Times,* was written when the demographers had established that if trends evident in 1972 continued, our population would eventually cease to increase. There follows a news item from the Washington *Post* reporting that these trends had not been interrupted as of the end of 1973. The concluding article in this section is an excerpt from a United States Census Bureau publication which reports (as of June 1973) the number of children women expect to have.

WHAT THE 1970 CENSUS SHOWED [1]

Today's average American is twenty-eight years old. How will that figure change by the year 2000? Will our society be younger or older?

Do more Americans live in our fifteen largest cities or in their suburbs?

Are white female college graduates apt to find better-paying jobs than their black counterparts?

[1] From "Surprises from the 1970 Census," by Trevor Armbrister, freelance writer. *Reader's Digest.* 103:135-9. Jl. '73. Reprinted with permission from the July 1973 *Reader's Digest.* Copyright 1973 by The Reader's Digest Assn., Inc.

Answers to these and numerous other questions about today's America are now available. Drawing upon the four billion facts collected in 1970, United States Census Bureau officials are painting an intriguing statistical portrait that contains a number of surprises about our society. To assess what lies behind the major changes currently taking place, I talked to bureau officials in Suitland, Maryland, and then set out across the country to interview some of the men and women whose life-styles the new statistics represent. Here's what I learned.

1. Our population growth rate has dropped markedly over the last decade to its lowest level in 150 years.

Soon after they married nine years ago, Bill and Ellen Peck of Baltimore, Maryland, decided not to have children. In fact, they helped to found the National Organization for Non-Parents, which today has branches in several states. "People shouldn't automatically assume that they must have children," the Pecks maintain. "Parenthood is a matter to be thought over carefully—for both the parents' sake and the child's."

Like the Pecks, more and more couples are opting against having children "automatically." Several factors are involved: rising costs, women's lib, the increasing number of working wives, the fact that women are staying single longer than ever before. Perhaps most important of all is the mounting concern over the effects of population growth on our environment.

Back in 1960, there were nearly 180 million Americans. Calculating that each family would continue to have three or more children, Census Bureau demographers projected that our population would exceed 300 million by the year 2000. By 1967, however, the birth rate had fallen to 2.9 children per family—and by the end of 1972 it had plummeted to 2. As a result of this unexpected drop, demographers have had to lower their projections for our year-2000 population by as much as 60 million.

Although the "baby boom" of the late 1950s continues

to crowd colleges, there . . . [were] 200,000 fewer first-grad-
ers in school this September [1973] than . . . [in 1972]—and
500,000 fewer than in 1970. The average American today
is twenty-eight years old, and there are twice as many people under fifteen as over sixty. By the year 2000, however,
that average age will rise to thirty-four, and the percentage
of our population under fifteen will drop significantly.

2. Americans are earning more than ever before, as the
shift away from blue-collar jobs accelerates.

For nearly twenty years, short, wiry Al Tardiff worked
as a lineman, truck driver and electrical meterman for
Florida Power & Light Company. Although he tried to better himself, the most he ever earned was $9000 per year.
Convinced that he had no future in a blue-collar job, he
enrolled at Palm Beach Junior College, transferring in 1969
to the school of hotel administration at the University of
Nevada. Today he's regional sales manager for Royal Inns
of America in Atlanta, Georgia, with a salary of $13,500
and ample fringe benefits. "Going back to college at the
age of thirty-nine," he says, "was the smartest decision I
ever made."

More and more Americans are following that path. In
1970, only 36 percent of all workers held blue-collar jobs
and that percentage is dropping rapidly. More than 50 percent of today's work force—up from 41 percent in 1960—is
engaged in what the Census Bureau calls "light labor" employment, and that figure is rising. In the service industries
(hotels, restaurants, recreation, etc.), 1972 alone witnessed
the creation of 440,000 new jobs.

Concurrent with this shift toward a service economy has
come a dramatic boost in personal income. In 1962, graduates with bachelor's degrees in accounting averaged offers
of $496 per month. Today those salaries have nearly dou-
bled to $886. Nowhere has this earnings jump been more
visible than in local, state and federal government jobs. As
recently as fifteen years ago, senior civil servants in Wash-

ington, D.C., earned $17,500 per year. Today, they may receive as much as $36,000.

What's encouraging about this increase is that it hasn't been restricted to white-collar or service-industry workers alone. Back in 1960, the average family-income (in terms of 1969 purchasing power) was $6,960. By 1971, it had reached $9,310. Census Bureau officials predict that by 1985 average family income will exceed $15,000.

3. The level of education is rising dramatically.

In a jumbo jet hurtling toward Los Angeles, thirty-seven-year-old physicist Clayne Yeates talked about his parents' belief in education. "They were always driving me, saying I had to study," he told me. Although Yeates' father went only as far as the tenth grade, all four of his sons earned college degrees—and Clayne went on to earn a doctorate.

Back in 1940, the median level of education was 8.4 years. Today it is 12.2, and still moving up. In 1970, 60 million Americans—more than a fourth of our population—were attending school. Today half of all Americans have completed high school, and a fourth have spent some time in college. Since 1940, the percentage holding degrees has doubled, from 6 to 12.

Affluence is one explanation for this spurt. Another is the mushrooming number of two-year colleges. Of the 943 two-year institutions operating today, at least 435 are less than ten years old—and their total enrollment now exceeds 1.9 million, with a prediction of 2.4 million by 1975.

4. Suburbs now exceed cities as the sites of jobs and homes.

For two and one half years, secretary Pam Grigsby battled traffic jams from her home in the suburbs to her Washington, D.C., office. The round trip took two hours or more, and parking cost between $40 and $45 per month. On one occasion vandals broke into her office. In 1971, her company moved out into suburban Maryland. Pam now drives to the office in less than thirty minutes, and parking in her building's garage costs just $22.50 per month. And she seldom worries about crime.

The pattern is the same everywhere. Between 1965 and 1970, the National Urban Coalition reports, New York City lost more than 13,000 manufacturing, retail, and wholesale businesses. Detroit lost 3,500, and Philadelphia nearly 3,000. Many relocated in suburbia, where large numbers of their workers already lived. In fact, more Americans now live in the suburbs (37.6 percent) than in the cities (31.5 percent), and many no longer commute. In the last decade alone, the proportion of those who chose to live *and* work in suburbia increased by 22 percent.

5. The status of women has changed dramatically.

In the fall of 1970, a willowy, twenty-six-year-old blonde named Patti Thibault took over as regional manager of the Charter Mortgage Company in Tustin, California. Not long afterward, she attended a meeting of fifteen building contractors. "It was the first time I noticed that I was a woman in the male business world," she says. "I asked a question, and the man answered not to me but to the man I was with."

As manager, Patti Thibault makes "between 50 and 200 decisions per week," involving hundreds of thousands of dollars in loans; she earns more than $20,000 per year in salary and commissions. "People are surprised to find that a woman is manager," she says, "especially one so young. But once they find out that you know your business, they accept you."

At the turn of the century, women constituted only 18 percent of the work force. Today they make up nearly 40 percent. Of the 12.7 million jobs added to the work force in the last decade, women accounted for 63.1 percent. As women's median level of education has risen, their earnings have multiplied correspondingly. Seven times as many women earn $10,000 or more today as did ten years ago, and nearly eight times as many earn between $7,000 and $10,000.

6. Minority groups have made striking gains.

"Dad kept saying a black man couldn't make it," recalls thirty-two-year-old Robert Archie of Las Vegas, Nevada. "But I was determined not to be as miserable as he was." After earning his bachelor's and law degrees, Archie served in Vietnam as an Army captain and returned home with a fistful of medals. A stint as a public defender brought him recognition, and in 1971 he was appointed director of Nevada's employment security department—the first black to hold a high cabinet position in the state. Today he earns $20,000 per year. "This job is a challenge," he says. "I want to prove that minorities and young people can do a job."

Between 1960 and 1970, the percentage of nonwhite families earning more than $10,000 (in terms of current purchasing power) increased from 13 to 30 percent. Black-family incomes are increasing even faster than white-family incomes, and the gains that black women have made are phenomenal. In 1960, for example, only 4,000 black women reported income of $10,000 or more. Today that total is above 100,000.

Just as significant has been the rise in the educational level of blacks. In 1940, they averaged 5.7 years of school; today, 10.3. Between 1964 and 1970, the number of blacks enrolled in college increased by 123 percent. Twice as many black men between the ages of twenty-five and twenty-nine boast a degree today as did ten years ago. The same is true for black women. In the north and west, black female college graduates actually earn more than their white counterparts.

THE BIRTHRATE FALLS [2]

"None Is Fun," read the lapel buttons sent out by mail.

"Stop at Two," say the leaflets handed out to motorists steaming in endless traffic jams.

[2] From "Each Change Has Vast Impact," by Jack Rosenthal, staff correspondent. New York *Times*. p E 9. Mr. 7, '73. © 1973 by The New York Times Company. Reprinted by permission.

"Zero population growth," urge thousands of members of the National ZPG movement that has, in four years, transformed demography from a dry, academic concern studded with soporific statistics into a topic of urgent public debate. . . .

With the publication of national vital statistics for 1972, it became evident that such efforts had been rewarded. The findings were unusually clear, even historic: The absolute number of births was the smallest in twenty-seven years. The birthrate dropped to its lowest level ever, declining 10 per cent just since 1971. And the fertility rate—the average number of children a woman has over her lifetime—plunged for the first time, below the symbolically important "replacement level" of . . . [2.11] children per family, averaging 2.03 for the year.

This was not zero population growth. For that to occur, very low fertility rates would have to persist for some seventy years—until existing bulges, like the post-World War II baby boom, work their way through the age structure of the population. No reputable authority would predict that such low rates will continue for long; fertility rates are notoriously volatile and unpredictable.

Nevertheless, the new statistics, showing an intensification of declines already evident in 1971, meant a period—perhaps a long period—of much slower national population growth. And that meant changes, in coming years, affecting almost every aspect of American society.

Most authorities believe these changes will be beneficial. They confidently dismiss fears, for example, that slow population growth will produce a stagnating economy.

In the first place, observes Michael F. Brewer, president of the Population Reference Bureau in Washington, the population—and demand—will still grow, even if more slowly. Further, average income will increase regardless of population size because of technological advancement. . . .

There would thus be less demand for school shoes but more of one for ski boots; a diminished market for baby food, but a growing one for gourmet restaurants; a smaller number of home buyers but a larger number of second-home owners.

Such economic gains and adaptations are likely to reinforce social changes. No one is sure whether women are having fewer children because they want to work or are working because they have fewer children. Either way, the proportion of women in the work force is rising steadily—adding further to average family income.

Another likely effect, indicated by findings of a National Fertility Study in 1970, is that fewer children mean fewer unwanted children. That, in turn, could well mean fewer poor children, whose presence dilutes family income and deters mothers from working.

Changes in education are already evident in empty primary-grade seats around the country. There were about four million first graders going to school in September 1968. The new figures mean that in 1978, there will be only about 3.2 million. And gradually the empty seats will be seen in progressively higher grades.

On the other hand, an ever-increasing proportion of teenagers is going on to community colleges. Adult education is booming.

The environmental impact of slower population growth is almost certain to be beneficial. Experts may argue about which factor puts more relative pressure on the environment, the size of the population or the affluence of the population. But there is no arguing that size is of some importance. . . . [A] presidential population commission estimated that fertility rates averaging two rather than three children per family would reduce the pressure on recreational facilities by as much as 30 per cent by the year 2000.

The impact of slower population growth on political life is imponderable. Slower growth certainly means older voters. According to one set of Census Bureau projections, the median age would rise from twenty-eight to thirty-six between 1972 and 2000. Slower growth appears to have brought rising conservatism in some countries like France, but not in others. Sweden remains in the forefront of social change. . . .

Well before the [ZPG] movement began, steady increases were evident in the number of women at work, later marriages, deferred births, divorces, abortions and women who want smaller families. At the same time, demographers credit the movement—and the parallel movements on behalf of the environment and women's liberation—with important attitudinal effects.

"We've been doing the right things," says Carl D. Pope, ZPG's Washington political director. "We've turned the population into something the man in the street can understand. And we took it to the grass-roots, to the neighborhoods. . . ."

The bomb is still there, ticking, in the current population. Since there are so many young women—children of the baby boom—now entering the child-bearing years, even a small increase in the fertility rate would bring an enormous increase in births. That is one of the dangers the ZPG movement will seek to guard against through continued public education and lobbying.

Another target is the unquestioned "growth mania" present for example in elementary school textbooks that often glorify large families but almost never depict happy singles.

In addition, says Judith Senderowitz, a ZPG vice president, "the mechanism to achieve ZPG—like available abortions and contraception, or removing conformist pressure to marry and have children almost automatically—is absolutely desirable and necessary even apart from the population problem. They are ways to increase personal freedom and improve the quality of life."

FERTILITY RATE STILL LOW [3]

The nation's population reached an estimated 211.7 million . . . [on January 1, 1974], the United States Census Bureau reported.

The total . . . represents a net gain of only 1.5 million over the figure . . . [for the previous year], compared with a net gain of 1.6 million during 1972 and 2 million in 1970.

A bureau spokesman said the declining increase corresponds with the nation's plummeting . . . [fertility] rate, which is now 2.08, or slightly below the 2.11 figure that is called the "replacement level." Several years ago the . . . [fertility] rate per couple was 2.7, which means that for every 10 couples, 27 children were born.

Replacement level is figured at 2.11 rather than an even 2 in order to compensate for the women who do not have children or who die in child-bearing years before they have had two children.

The nation's net gain in population is less than half the highest gain ever recorded—3.1 million in 1956.

The rate of gain during 1973 was 0.7 per cent, compared with 0.8 per cent in 1971. From 1947 to 1961, during the so-called baby boom, the annual rate of gain ranged from 1.6 to 1.8 per cent.

In 1973, according to Census estimates, the net gain resulted from about 3.2 million births, 2 million deaths, and a net immigration of 350,000.

WOMEN'S BIRTH EXPECTATIONS [4]

In June 1973, as in June 1972, young wives in the eighteen- to twenty-four-year age group anticipated an average completed family size of about 2.3 children. This contrasts

[3] Article, "Population Hits 211 Million." Washington *Post.* p 18. Ja. 1, '74. © 1974 by The Washington Post. Reprinted by permission.
[4] From *Birth Expectations of American Wives, June 1973.* (United States. Bureau of the Census. Current Population Reports: Population Characteristics. Series P-20, no 254) Supt. of Docs. Washington, D.C. 20402. '73. p. 1.

markedly with an average anticipation of 2.9 found for young wives in a 1967 survey and with 3.1 in 1965. These data confirm that young wives now expect an average family size that is at or near the replacement level.

Replacement-level fertility refers to the average number of children required to replace the persons of one generation with those of the next, allowing for those who will die before reaching the age of their mother at the time of their birth. At current levels of mortality, replacement-level fertility is estimated to be approximately 2.1 children per woman (including single women), but 2.2 per wife. (Approximately 95 percent of all women become wives. Replacement-level fertility, if maintained, would, in the absence of net immigration from abroad, lead to zero population growth.)

Birth expectations among young Negro wives appear to have reached a level which closely parallels that of young white wives. The data show, however, that the young Negro wives have already had more births to date than the white wives. Moreover, Negroes have historically had higher levels of fertility than white women of the same age. It remains to be seen, therefore, whether or not the similarity of expectations will lead to similarity in accomplished fertility in the years to come.

For the first time . . . data have been developed for women of Spanish origin. The results show that the eighteen- to twenty-four-year-old wives in this ethnic group expect an average of about 2.6 children per wife. This contrasts with an expected average family size of 3.7 for Spanish-origin wives in the thirty to thirty-nine age group.

The distribution of reporting wives according to the number of children expected when their family is completed shows that about 70 percent of the wives eighteen- to twenty-four-years old in 1973 expected to have *no more than two children*. This figure also is in marked contrast to expectations recorded in 1967, when the comparable figure was 45 percent. Among older women expectations of completed-family size involve the fact that most of the children have already been born. In the still highly fertile age group twenty-five- to twenty-nine-years old, 63 percent of the wives expect a completed-family size of two children or less, up from 37 percent in 1967. For wives thirty-five- to thirty-nine-years old at the survey dates, the percentage expecting no more than two children has remained almost constant since 1967 at 37 or 38 percent.

The level of a woman's educational attainment has in the past been a very strong differentiating factor in terms of her accomplished fertility. Women of lower educational attainment have, on the average, more children than women with considerable education. This pattern is reflected in the expectations of women regarding their future fertility, particularly among older women whose lifetime fertility is largely completed. Among younger wives, however, expectations for the future show a much narrower range among the educational levels. Wives eighteen- to twenty-four-years old show an average expected-family size of 2.1 children for women with some college, whereas women with less than a complete high school education expect an average family size of 2.4. Given sampling variability, the true difference could be narrower or wider than that indicated. An additional point worth noting in connection with expectations by educational attainment is that women under thirty with a college education may fall short of replacing themselves. The fact that a slightly higher percentage of college women have tended to remain unmarried and the relatively small families expected by the married college women lend credence to such an observation.

The low levels of expected future fertility among America's young wives suggests that the current low birthrates will remain low for the immediate future at least.

II. CONTROVERSIES AND POLICIES

EDITOR'S INTRODUCTION

In this section the accent is on controversies about population policies. The section starts with an excerpt from President Nixon's Message to Congress in which he called for the setting up of a commission to examine what should be done about America's population growth. A digest of the commission's report, favoring an eventual stabilization of US population, follows. Among the recommendations were free access to contraceptives for sexually active teenagers and, in effect, abortion on demand. Next is presented a report of President Nixon's negative reaction to these two recommendations and his silence about other Commission proposals.

One of the important factors producing a growing population is immigration. In an article from the New York *Times Magazine,* Leslie Aldridge Westoff argues that we should cut severely the number of immigrants allowed into the country.

The next selection is Planned Parenthood's 1972 statement on population which calls for working towards the goal of a nation of "stable size"—eventual stabilization of our numbers. This is followed by Zero Population Growth's statement of its aims—a stable population by 1990 and a reduction in population thereafter. ZPG formulates definite aims; the Population Commission has a more general approach. ZPG is critically examined in the succeeding article, from *Daedalus,* by the demographer Kingsley Davis, who shows what is involved in ZPG's demands and how to ensure a stable population. Also from *Daedalus* is an excerpt from an article by John P. Holdren which points out the increasing strain on our resources that a growing population creates.

On the other hand, Amitai Etzioni, writing in *Evaluation,* casts doubt on the desirability of ZPG's aims. He believes we may find moderate growth better than zero growth. The final selection in this section is an extract from a pamphlet published by the League of Women Voters, pointing out that the United States, in spite of all the discussion of population matters, has no population policy.

PRESIDENT NIXON ON POPULATION [1]

To the Congress of the United States:

In 1830 there were one billion people on the planet earth. By 1930 there were two billion, and by 1960 there were three billion. Today the world population is three and one-half billion persons.

These statistics illustrate the dramatically increasing rate of population growth. It took many thousands of years to produce the first billion people; the next billion took a century; the third came after thirty years; the fourth will be produced in just fifteen.

If this rate of population growth continues, it is likely that the earth will contain over seven billion human beings by the end of this century. Over the next thirty years, in other words, the world's population could double. And at the end of that time, each new addition of one billion persons would not come over the millennia nor over a century nor even over a decade. If present trends were to continue until the year 2000, the eighth billion would be added in only five years and each additional billion in an even shorter period.

While there are a variety of opinions as to precisely how fast population will grow in the coming decades, most in-

[1] From *Established Population Growth Commission: Message from the President of the United States Relative to Population Growth.* (House Document no. 91-139) 91st Congress; 1st session. U.S. Gov. Ptg. Office. Washington, D.C. 20401. '69. p 1, 3-5+.

formed observers have a similar response to all such projections. They agree that population growth is among the most important issues we face. They agree that it can be met only if there is a great deal of advance planning. And they agree that the time for such planning is growing very short. It is for all these reasons that I address myself to the population problem in this message. . . .

For some time population growth has been seen as a problem for developing countries. Only recently has it come to be seen that pressing problems are also posed for advanced industrial countries when their populations increase at the rate that the United States, for example, must now anticipate. Food supplies may be ample in such nations, but social supplies—the capacity to educate youth, to provide privacy and living space, to maintain the processes of open, democratic government—may be grievously strained.

In the United States our rate of population growth is not as great as that of developing nations. In this country, in fact, the growth rate has generally declined since the eighteenth century. The present growth rate of about 1 percent per year is still significant, however. . . .

Several factors contribute to the yearly increase, including the large number of couples of childbearing age, the typical size of American families, and our increased longevity. We are rapidly reaching the point in this country where a family reunion, which has typically brought together children, parents, and grandparents, will instead gather family members from *four* generations. This is a development for which we are grateful and of which we can be proud. But we must also recognize that it will mean a far larger population if the number of children born to each set of parents remains the same.

In 1917 the total number of Americans passed 100 million, after three full centuries of steady growth. In 1967—just half a century later—the 200 million mark was passed. If the present rate of growth continues, the third hundred-million persons will be added in roughly a thirty-year pe-

riod. This means that by the year 2000, or shortly thereafter, there will be more than 300 million Americans.

This growth will produce serious challenges for our society. I believe that many of our present social problems
may be related to the fact that we have had only fifty years
in which to accommodate the second hundred-million Americans. In fact, since 1945 alone some 90 million babies have
been born in this country. We have thus had to accomplish
in a very few decades an adjustment to population growth
which was once spread over centuries. And it now appears
that we will have to provide for a third hundred-million
Americans in a period of just thirty years.

The great majority of the next hundred-million Americans will be born to families which looked forward to their
birth and are prepared to love them and care for them as
they grow up. The critical issue is whether social institutions will also plan for their arrival and be able to accommodate them in a humane and intelligent way. We can be
sure that society will *not* be ready for this growth unless it
begins its planning immediately. And adequate planning,
in turn, requires that we ask ourselves a number of important questions.

Where, for example, will the next hundred-million
Americans live? If the patterns of the last few decades hold
for the rest of the century, then at least three quarters of
the next hundred-million persons will locate in highly ur-
banized areas. Are our cities prepared for such an influx?
The chaotic history of urban growth suggests that they are
not and that many of their existing problems will be severely aggravated by a dramatic increase in numbers. Are
there ways, then, of readying our cities? Alternatively, can
the trend toward greater concentration of population be
reversed? Is it a desirable thing, for example, that half of
all the counties in the United States actually lost population in the 1950s, despite the growing number of inhabitants in the country as a whole? Are there ways of fostering
a better distribution of the growing population?

Some have suggested that systems of satellite cities or completely new towns can accomplish this goal. The National Commission on Urban Growth has . . . produced a stimulating report on this matter, one which recommends the creation of one hundred new communities averaging 100,000 people each, and ten new communities averaging at least one million persons. But the total number of people who would be accommodated if even this bold plan were implemented is only twenty million—a mere one fifth of the expected thirty-year increase. If we were to accommodate the full 100 million persons in new communities, we would have to build a new city of 250,000 persons each month from now until the end of the century. That means constructing a city the size of Tulsa, Dayton, or Jersey City every thirty days for over thirty years. Clearly, the problem is enormous, and we must examine the alternative solutions very carefully.

Other questions also confront us. How, for example, will we house the next hundred-million Americans? Already economical and attractive housing is in very short supply. New architectural forms, construction techniques, and financing strategies must be aggressively pioneered if we are to provide the needed dwellings.

What of our natural resources and the quality of our environment? Pure air and water are fundamental to life itself. Parks, recreational facilities, and an attractive countryside are essential to our emotional well-being. Plant and animal and mineral resources are also vital. A growing population will increase the demand for such resources. But in many cases their supply will not be increased and may even be endangered. The ecological system upon which we now depend may seriously deteriorate if our efforts to conserve and enhance the environment do not match the growth of the population.

How will we educate and employ such a large number of people? Will our transportation systems move them about as quickly and economically as necessary? How will we provide adequate health care when our population reaches 300 million? Will our political structures have to be reordered, too, when our society grows to such proportions? Many of our institutions are already under tremendous strain as they try to respond to the demands of 1969. Will they be swamped by a growing flood of people in the next thirty years? How easily can they be replaced or altered?

Finally we must ask: how can we better assist American families so that they will have no more children than they wish to have? In my first message to Congress on domestic affairs, I called for a national commitment to provide a healthful and stimulating environment for all children during their first five years of life. One of the ways in which we can promote that goal is to provide assistance for more parents in effectively planning their families. We know that involuntary childbearing often results in poor physical and emotional health for all members of the family. It is one of the factors which contribute to our distressingly high infant-mortality rate, the unacceptable level of malnutrition, and the disappointing performance of some children in our schools. Unwanted or untimely childbearing is one of several forces which are driving many families into poverty or keeping them in that condition. Its threat helps to produce the dangerous incidence of illegal abortion. And finally, of course, it needlessly adds to the burdens placed on all our resources by increasing population.

None of the questions I have raised here is new. But all of these questions must now be asked and answered with a new sense of urgency. The answers cannot be given by government alone, nor can government alone turn the answers into programs and policies. I believe, however, that the Federal Government does have a special responsibility for defining these problems and for stimulating thoughtful responses. . . .

It is for all these reasons that I today propose the cre-

ation by Congress of a Commission on Population Growth
and the American Future. . . .

One of the most serious challenges to human destiny in
the last third of this century will be the growth of the
population. Whether man's response to that challenge will
be a cause for pride or for despair in the year 2000 will depend very much on what we do today. If we now begin our
work in an appropriate manner, and if we continue to
devote a considerable amount of attention and energy to
this problem, then mankind will be able to surmount this
challenge as it has surmounted so many during the long
march of civilization.

POPULATION COMMISSION REPORT [2]

A conscious government policy to help "improve the
quality of life" by gradually slowing and eventually halting
US population growth was recommended by the Commission on Population Growth and the American Future. The
Commission's final report was delivered to the President
and the Congress in March [1972] after two years of de-
liberation. The 24-member panel pointed out that "at a
minimum, we will probably add 50 million more Americans
by the end of the century" as an echo-effect of the post-
World War II "baby boom." Beyond that, the Commission
held, continued growth would confer no possible benefit to
the nation or its people, while it would aggravate some of
our most pressing social and economic problems. Slower
growth, the Commission stated, will not eliminate these
problems, "but it will reduce the urgency, the 'crash program' character of much that we do. It will buy time for the
development of sensible solutions."

The Commission members emphasized that while slower
growth "provides opportunities, it does not guarantee that

[2] From "Population and the American Future: The Commission's Final Report," by Richard Lincoln, staff editor. *Family Planning Perspectives.* 4:10-15+.
Ap. '72. Reprinted with permission from *Family Planning Perspectives,* v 4, no
2, April 1972.

they will be well used. It simply opens up a range of choices we would not have otherwise. . . . Successfully addressing population requires that we also address our problems of poverty, of minority and sex discrimination, of careless exploitation of resources, of environmental deterioration, and of spreading suburbs, decaying cities, and wasted countrysides."

The Commission pointed out that the country could "cope with rapid population growth for the next thirty to fifty years. But doing so will become an increasingly unpleasant and risky business . . . adopting solutions we don't like . . . before we understand them."

The Commission, therefore, called upon the nation to "welcome and plan for a stabilized population," emphasizing that "achievement of population stabilization would be primarily the result of measures aimed at creating conditions in which individuals, regardless of sex, age, or minority status, can exercise genuine free choice. This means that we must strive to eliminate those social barriers, laws, and cultural pressures that interfere with the exercise of free choice and that governmental programs in the future must be sensitized to demographic effects."

While advocating an eventual *average* two-child family, the panel stated that this average could—and ought only— be obtained by voluntary means with "respect for human freedom, human dignity, and individual fulfillment; and concern for social justice and social welfare. To 'solve' population problems at the cost of such values would be a Pyrrhic victory. . . ."

Diversity Encouraged

The Commission indicated that an average two-child family may be achieved "by varying combinations of nonmarriage or childlessness" combined with "substantial percentages of couples who have more than two children." The Commission found it "desirable" that stabilization be attained "in a way which encourages variety and choice rather than uniformity."

In the long run, *average* zero population growth, the panel pointed out, "can only be achieved . . . with fluctuations in both directions." If, through individual informed free choice, the population grows at less than the replacement level for a period of time "we should prepare ourselves not to react with alarm, as some other countries have done recently [e.g., Japan and Rumania] when the distant possibility of population decline appears." Indeed, the Commissioners found, "there might be no reason to fear a decline in population once we are past the period of growth that is in store," and, "in any event it is naive to expect that we can fine-tune such trends." Certainly, we should not withhold the means to prevent or terminate unwanted pregnancies since "a nation's growth should not depend on the ignorance or misfortune of its citizenry."

Of the many possible paths to achievement of population stabilization, the Commission stated its preference for a gradual course "which minimizes fluctuations in the number of births; minimizes further growth of population; minimizes the change required in reproductive habits and provides adequate time for such changes to be adopted; and maximizes variety and choice in life styles, while minimizing pressures for conformity." Population stabilization could not be reached quickly, the panel pointed out, without social and economic disruption caused by an "accordion-like continuous expansion and contraction" of average-family size over the next several decades.

One such "optimal path," which could achieve replacement fertility in twenty years and population stabilization at 278 million in fifty years (excluding the effect of immigration), would involve:

a decline in the proportion of women becoming mothers from 88 to 80 percent

a decline in the proportion of parents with three or more children from 50 to 41 percent

an increase in the proportion of parents with one or
two children from 50 to 59 percent

an increase of two years in the average age at which a
mother bears her first child

an increase of less than six months in the average inter-
val between births

Building on Current Trends

The Commission found cause for belief that "something
close to an optimal path can be realized" providing that
deliberate action which can encourage desirable trends is
taken quickly. Favorable developments cited by the panel
include: a historic long-term decline in average-family size
(temporarily interrupted by the post-World War II baby
boom); continued birthrate declines over the last decade
despite the coming to reproductive age of the baby-boom
babies; improvements in the employment and social status
of women; mounting public concern over the negative effects of population growth; a decline in the number of
youthful marriages; preference by younger couples for
smaller families than their elders desired; improved effectiveness of contraceptives; increased access to legal abortions; the experience of at least ten other countries which
have, in the last half-century, experienced periods of replacement fertility.

The panel warned, however, that if its recommendations
were not adopted quickly, instead of encouraging a desirable trend "we may find ourselves in a position of trying
to reverse an undesirable trend."

The Commission cited several "unfavorable elements
which threaten the achievement of stabilization," including
the potential for a repeat baby boom; our "ideological addiction to growth"; "pronatalist" laws [laws that encourage
child bearing] and social institutions, including mass media
projections of stereotypical women's roles; restrictions on
availability of contraception, sex education and abortion
[the United States Supreme Court legalized abortion within

the first six months of pregnancy in 1973]; reawakened fear of "race suicide," such as occurred during the Depression.

Action now is also important, the report stated, because the 1970s are probably a "critical . . . decade in the demographic transition . . . involving changes in family life and the role of women, dynamics of the metropolitan process, the depopulation of rural areas, the movement and the needs of disadvantaged minorities, the era of the young adults produced by the baby boom, and the attendant question of what their own fertility will be—baby boom or baby bust."

Policy Recommendations

The Commission indicated that it sought to make policy recommendations which were technically, politically and economically feasible; recommendations which, while speaking to population issues, embodied goals "either intrinsically desirable or worthwhile for reasons other than demographic objectives."

To move the nation toward realization of these goals, the Commission assessed a broad range of current policies and programs and recommended a comprehensive set of changes in existing policies or adoption of new policies. The Commission's principal recommendations called for:

elimination of involuntary childbearing by substantially improving the access of all Americans (regardless of marital or socioeconomic status) to effective means of fertility control

the improvement of the status of women

more education about population, parenthood, sex, nutrition, environment and heredity

maintenance of foreign immigration levels, and more rational guidance of internal migration to metropolitan areas

increased biomedical research in human reproduction and contraceptive development . . .

Involuntary Childbearing

Some dozen of the Commission's major recommendations were designed to enable "all Americans, regardless of age, marital status, or income . . . to avoid unwanted births." The panel pointed out that while most couples plan to have between two and three children, because of "youthful marriage, far-from-perfect means of fertility control, and varying motivation, many of these couples will have children before they want them and a significant fraction will ultimately exceed the number they want." Citing the 1970 National Fertility Study, the panel pointed out that of all births to currently married women between 1966 and 1970, "15 percent were reported by the parents as having never been wanted." An additional 29 percent were reported as having been born before the parents wanted them. Thus, a total of 44 percent of all births to married couples in those five years were unplanned. The Commission made a "conservative" estimate from these findings that "2.65 million births occurring in that five-year period would never have occurred had the complete availability of perfect fertility control permitted couples to realize their preferences." The panel pointed out that the incidence of unwanted fertility, with its "enormous" financial, social, health and psychological costs, remained highest for the poor and the poorly educated. "Mainly because of differences in education and income—and a general exclusion from the socioeconomic mainstream—unwanted fertility weighs most heavily on certain minority groups," such as blacks and, "probably," Puerto Ricans, Mexican Americans and Indians, as well. (Thus, the panel reported, "if blacks could have the number of children they want and no more, their fertility and that of the majority white population would be very similar.")

While only 1 percent of the first births were reported by their parents as having never been wanted, nearly two thirds of sixth and higher order births were so reported;

these births were concentrated in the later years of child-bearing, the Commission found, where mother and child are at greatest risk of death or damage. Eliminating unwanted births in the older ages would also sharply reduce the incidence of such hereditary diseases as mongolism. Similarly, the Commission pointed out, 17 percent of all births occur to teenagers at a time when the likelihood of adverse health and social consequences for mother and infant is much greater than if the birth were postponed to the years between twenty and thirty-five. The postponement of these early mistimed births to later ages could result in a "distinct improvement in the survival, health, and ability" of the children born.

So "that only wanted children are brought into the world," the Commission adopted a series of recommendations to:

provide full financing of all health services related to fertility. . . .

extend the family-planning-project grant programs

eliminate legal restrictions on access to contraceptive information and services

increase investment in reproductive research and contraceptive development

eliminate administrative restrictions on voluntary contraceptive sterilization. . . .

develop programs of family-planning education

Legal Restrictions

Twenty-two states have laws restricting or regulating the sale, distribution, advertising or display of contraceptives, and six more have restrictions on selling or advertising prophylactics. These laws range from prohibition of contraceptive sales to the unmarried in Massachusetts and Wisconsin (recently declared unconstitutional by the United States Supreme Court) to laws prohibiting sale of contraceptives or prophylactics through vending machines, adver-

tising them on outdoor billboards or even displaying them
in drugstores. The Commission held that such laws "inhibit
family-planning education as well as family-planning programs, and/or impinge on the ready availability of methods
of contraception to the public. By prohibiting commercial
sales, advertising displays, and the use of vending machines
for nonprescription contraceptives, they sacrifice accessibil-
ity, education, and individual rights. . . ."

The Commission recommended that states not only
"eliminate existing legal inhibitions and restrictions on access to contraceptive information, procedures, and supplies," but "develop statutes affirming the desirability that
all persons have ready and practicable access" to them.

The Commission pointed out that some three million
couples in the childbearing years had, by 1970, elected contraceptive sterilization; this comprised nearly one in five
couples able to bear children who did not want to have any
more. Despite the great—and increasing—popularity of this
method of family limitation, the Commission pointed out
that many physicians would not perform such operations
because of fear that they might be sued or prosecuted, and
many hospitals imposed requirements limiting the operation to persons of specified age or previous parity [the state
of having borne children]. The Commission recommended
that all such requirements be eliminated so that the decision for contraceptive sterilization "be made solely by the
physician and patient."

The Commission found [before the Supreme Court de-
cision], that "the various prohibitions against abortion
throughout the United States stand as obstacles to the exercise of individual freedom: the freedom of women to make
difficult moral choices based on their personal values, the
freedom of women to control their own fertility, and finally,
freedom from the burdens of unwanted childbearing." The
Commission also held that such prohibitions "violate social
justice," forcing women to bear unwanted children, or to
undergo dangerous and illegal abortions to avert unwanted

births, with less burden on the rich woman—who has had access to medically safe, and expensive, abortions—than the poor woman, "forced to risk her life and health with folk remedies and disreputable practitioners."

The Commission stated that "abortion on request" in New York, California and eastern European countries brought the procedure "from the backrooms to the hospitals and clinics" with consequent reductions in illegal abortions and resultant maternal mortality. (Thus, in New York City, maternal mortality rates "dropped by two-thirds the year after abortion became available on request . . . [and] there is reason to suspect that the maternal death ratio will continue to decline.") The Commission also pointed to evidence that New York's abortion law had sharply reversed illegitimacy rates, which had been rising since first recorded in 1954. (There were nearly 10 percent fewer out-of-wedlock births for the first nine months of 1971 in New York City as compared to the same months in 1970.)

Legalizing abortion would also "exert a downward influence on the United States birthrate," the Commission predicted, based on the evidence in New York City. (New York showed a 12 percent decline in births in 1971 over 1970—three times the national decline.) The panel warned that "abortion should not be considered a substitute for birth control, but rather as one element in a comprehensive system of maternal and infant health care." It affirmed that "contraception is the method of choice for preventing an unwanted birth," and predicted that "with the increasing availability of contraceptives and improvements in contraceptive technology, the need for abortion will diminish." . . . However, the more than half-million legal abortions and "an unknown number of illegal abortions" performed in the year ending June 30, 1971, indicate that there is still a widespread "social and personal failure in the provision and use of birth control," and many Americans still "must resort to abortion to prevent an unwanted birth."

For these reasons, the majority of the Commissioners affirmed that "women should be free to determine their own fertility, that the matter of abortion should be left to the conscience of the individual concerned, in consultation with her physician and that states should be encouraged to enact affirmative statutes creating a clear and positive framework for the practice of abortion on request." . . .

The Commission . . . recommended that "federal, state, and local governments make funds available to support abortion services . . . [and] that abortion be specifically included in comprehensive health insurance benefits, both public and private."

Dissents from the majority recommendation on abortion—on various grounds—were registered by five of the twenty-four-member panel. . . .

Reproductive, Contraceptive Research

Unwanted pregnancies will continue to occur, the Commission declared, until methods of fertility control are made universally available which are "safe and free of any adverse reactions; effective, acceptable, coitus-independent, and accessible commercially rather than medically; and inexpensive, easy to use, and reversible. This goal will be reached only if research efforts equal the magnitude of the task." The report stated that while the pill and the IUD [intrauterine device] "represented significant breakthroughs in a field which has been largely neglected by science for most of human history," in terms of the potential technology which should be feasible, these methods remain "fairly primitive." This, the Commission said, is because "our knowledge of basic reproductive biology is inadequate." We do not yet know "the role and functioning of the ovary and the testes, of the egg and the sperm, of the process of fertilization itself, and the normal course of gestation." In addition to such basic investigation, far more effort than is currently being expended must be devoted to development of new contraceptive methods and evaluation of the safety and effectiveness of existing ones. The Commission found the $75 million for 1973 research expenditures projected by DHEW's [Department of Health, Education, and Welfare] Five-Year Plan "modest" in terms of the need, but "far above the total amounts requested" for this purpose by DHEW—only $44.8 million for FY [Fiscal Year] 1973. "This amount is far too small," the panel declared, "for a task which is crucial . . . in dealing with the population problem. . . ." The Commission projected that at least $250 million annually would be needed for population-related research: $100 million (in federal funds) for basic biomedical research in human reproduction, $100 million (mostly in federal funds) for developmental work on methods of fertility control, and at least $50 million (in federal funds) for behavioral and operational research.

The Commission recommended that "this nation give the highest priority to research in reproductive biology and to the search for improved methods by which individuals can control their own fertility." The panel called for the appropriation and allocation in FY 1973 of "the full $93 million authorized for this purpose," rising to "a minimum of $150 million by 1975; and that private organizations continue and expand their work in this field."

Unwanted Births and the Poor

The 1965 and 1970 National Fertility Studies showed that while all socioeconomic groups experience unwanted pregnancies, "they occur most often and have the most serious consequences among low-income couples." Since 1967, the Commission report pointed out, the federal government has sought to increase the availability of family planning to low-income couples, largely through project grant programs carried out by DHEW's National Center for Family Planning Services and by the Office of Economic Opportunity [OEO] "With a relatively modest federal investment, organized family-planning programs have succeeded in introducing modern family-planning services to nearly 40 percent of low-income persons in need." To reach the majority of those in need who remain unserved, the Commission reported, "will clearly require additional federal authorizations and appropriations as well as increased support for these programs from state and local governments, and from private philanthropy." The Commission estimated that perhaps $50 million annually might be forthcoming for family-planning services from state and local governments and private sources and urged more financial support from these sources; the bulk of the funds, however, will have to come from the DHEW and OEO project grant programs. Specifically, the Commission recommended new legislation to extend the current family-planning-project grant program under Title X of the Public Health Service Act. . . . It also recommended maintenance of the project grant authority under Title V of the Social Security Act . . . , and continuation of OEO family-planning programs "at current levels of authorization." . . .

The Commission urged that "no means test be applied in the administration of these programs. Their purpose must be to enlarge personal freedom for all, not to restrict its benefits only to the poorest of the poor." The Commission pointed out that "there are many nonpoor individuals who need but who do not receive adequate fertility control services" who may become poor through unwanted childbearing if they are denied services.

The panel considered and rejected proposals to revise tax policies, or provide financial incentives—or disincentives—to encourage couples to have small families, or to discourage them from having large families. "Clearly, no proposal to penalize childbearing or reward nonchildbearing can be acceptable in a situation in which fertility control is not completely reliable and large numbers of unwanted births occur." The Commission pointed out that, in practice, proposed bonus payments for not bearing children, and withdrawal of public benefits from those who bear too many, have been directed toward the poor, and "almost without exception . . . toward one group—welfare recipients."

What is more, all proposals to penalize childbearing—even those not specifically directed at the poor—"have the effect of penalizing the child and his siblings."

In addition to dismissing such proposals on the grounds of social equity, the Commission dismissed the frequently asserted claim that "because assistance payments are based upon the number of children in the family, welfare mothers have more children in order to increase their monthly payment." The panel added that there is no "evidence that present tax policies and public expenditures promote the birth of additional children in any social class." Rather, the Commission found, "the reverse might be true." As an example, the panel cited the fact that births to welfare mothers in New York City declined from 18.9 percent in 1959, when payments were low, to 11.3 percent in 1970 when the payments were much higher; and for the nation as a whole the average-family size of welfare recipients declined between 1967 and 1969, a period when welfare payments were increasing.

The Commission also reviewed—and rejected—various proposals to require parents to assume all or a greater proportion of the costs of their children by withdrawing subsidies for education, health and social services; levying a fee for childbearing or providing a bonus for not having children; or relieving nonparents of some or all of the tax costs of education, health and other services for children. "The only reason to alter present policies which are supportive of children," the panel said, "would be if an even higher good were to be served. We cannot foresee any goal with a higher priority than insuring the welfare of future generations."

Fertility-Related Health Services

In order that "future generations of Americans . . . be born wanted by their parents, brought into the world with the best skills that modern medicine can offer, and provided with the love and care necessary for a healthy and productive life," the Commission recommended "a national policy and voluntary program to reduce unwanted fertility, to improve the outcome of pregnancy, and to improve the health of children." . . .

The Commission estimated the total cost for such a program to range from $6.7 to $8.1 billion annually in the next five years, but pointed out that all but about $1 billion of this total cost is already being financed (although these critical services are distributed unevenly, with many persons receiving only some of them or receiving services of poor quality).

The Commission added that the "costs . . . would, in all probability, be more than offset by the benefits to individuals and society of the delivery of healthy children and the prevention of unwanted pregnancies." The panel held that the financing of these services "could easily be integrated into current publicly administered health financing systems, and made part of a new comprehensive national health insurance system. Congress should include this coverage in any health insurance system it adopts."

Covering the costs of such a program would not guarantee the delivery of these services to those in need of them, the Commission pointed out, declaring that "systematic attention" must also be given "to the organization and delivery" of the services. To accomplish this, the Commission recommended that programs be created to train doctors, nurses and paraprofessionals in the provision of all fertility-related health services, develop new patterns for the use of such personnel, evaluate improved methods of organizing service delivery, and establish the capacity to provide services in areas which have few health resources.

Teenage Services and Education

A number of the recommendations in the Commission report were addressed to meeting the health and social problems leading to and resulting from adolescent pregnancy.

The Commission cited a recent national study by Drs. John Kantner and Melvin Zelnick of Johns Hopkins University, which showed that 27 percent of unwed girls fifteen to nineteen years of age had already experienced some sexual intercourse. This rose from 14 percent of fifteen-year-old girls to 44 percent of nineteen-year-olds. Only 20 percent of sexually active teenage girls used contraceptives regularly, with the majority using them not at all or seldom (although almost all of them had heard about the pill). "Such a low incidence of contraceptive use," the report stated, "is particularly significant when less than half of these girls knew when during the monthly cycle a girl can become pregnant." Significant rates of sexual activity and little use of contraception among teenagers has led to rising rates of adolescent pregnancy, venereal disease, illegitimacy, forced (and unstable) marriage and recourse to abortion, the report stated.

The Commission pointed to the fact that out-of-wedlock adolescent birthrates had increased as much as threefold between 1940 and 1968 and venereal disease had become "epidemic." In 1968 more than 600,000 infants—17 percent of all births—were born to teenagers; and one fourth of girls who recently reached their twentieth birthday had already borne a child. At best, the Commission pointed out, adolescent pregnancy—especially in the early teens—involves serious health and social consequences—far more severe than for women over twenty. The infants of these young mothers "are subject to higher risks of prematurity, mortality, and serious physical and intellectual impairments than are children of mothers twenty to thirty-five." Those girls who bear a first child at an early age—inside or outside of marriage—tend to bear subsequent children at a rapid rate. ("Sixty percent of girls who had a child before the age of sixteen had another baby while still of school age.") Education and employment opportunities of these girls are likely to be seriously impaired. ("Pregnancy is the number one cause for school dropout among females in the United States.") The psychological effects, the report states, "are indicated by a recent study that estimated that teenage mothers have a suicide rate ten times that of the general population."

The Commission attributed much of the recent rise in adolescent pregnancy—with all its attendant social and health problems—to the denial of accurate information about sexuality, parenthood and birth control and the inaccessibility of effective birth control services.

The Commission was highly critical of those "well-organized and vocal" opponents of sex education who, to the panel members' "regret," had "successfully forestalled sex education in thirteen states." Keeping youngsters in ignorance, the Commission members stated, "does not serve to prevent sexual activity, but rather promotes the undesirable consequences of sexual behavior—unwanted pregnancy, unwanted maternity, and venereal disease."

The Commission urged that "funds be made available to the National Institute of Mental Health to support the development of a variety of model programs in human sexuality" based both in schools and the community. The panel recommended that "sex education be made available to all, and that it be presented in a responsible manner through community organizations, the media and especially the schools." Because of the "serious social and health consequences involved in teenage pregnancy and the high rates of teenage out-of-wedlock pregnancy and venereal disease," the Commission also urged "the elimination of legal restrictions on access to contraceptive and prophylactic information and services by young people." It recommended that "states adopt affirmative legislation" permitting minors to receive such information and services "in appropriate settings sensitive to their needs and concerns." . . .

The Commission urged that not only should "birth control services and information be made available to teenagers . . . regardless of age, marital status, or number of children," but that there be implemented "an adequately financed program to develop appropriate family-planning materials, to conduct training courses for teachers and school administrators, and to assist states and local communities in integrating information about family planning into school courses such as hygiene and sex education."

While stressing "the necessity of minimizing adolescent pregnancy by making contraceptive information and services available" to sexually active youth, the Commission urged that adolescents who do become pregnant "not be stigmatized and removed from society." It urged that "school systems . . . make certain that pregnant adolescents have the opportunity to continue their education, and that they are aided in gaining access to adequate health, nutritional, and counseling services." It also held that the "word *illegitimate* and the stigma attached to it have no place in our society." The panel recommended that "all children, regardless of the circumstances of their birth, be accorded fair and equal status, socially, morally, and legally." It called for "revision of those laws and practices which result in discrimination against out-of-wedlock children."

Education in Population, Family Life and Human Reproduction

In addition to sex and birth control education, the Commission made numerous other recommendations in the educational field to help young people "make rational, informed decisions about their own and their descendants' future. . . ."

The Commission called for a program of population education to provide young people with "knowledge about population processes, population characteristics, the causes of population change, and the consequences of such change for the individual and for the society." The Commission could find "no evidence that anything approaching an adequate population program now exists in our schools. Very few teachers are trained in the subject and textual materials are scant and inadequate." . . .

The Commission recommended the enactment of a Population Education Act "to assist school systems in establishing well-planned population education programs so that present and future generations will be better prepared to meet the challenges arising from population change." . . .

At the college level, the Commission urged that population study be included in all introductory social science courses.

The panel advocated education for parenthood, encompassing "a diversity of styles of family life in America today," including acceptance "without stigma" of those individuals who choose to remain childless. It urged that young people be made aware of the real costs of raising children, both emotional and financial (the latter estimated to average $60,000 from birth through college for a first child): "With some idea of the financial demands of children, parents can plan ahead and be better prepared to provide the kind of life they want for their children."

The Commission chided the mass media for depicting family life in a way that "bears little resemblance to that experienced by most of the population," and urged the media ("a potent educational force . . . American children and adults spend an estimated average of twenty-seven hours a week watching television") to "assume more responsibility in presenting information and education for family living to the public." The Commission also called on community agencies, "especially the school," to assume a more active and more sensitive role in education for parenthood, and that financial support be provided for such programs by DHEW.

The panel, citing estimates that one in fifteen children may be born with "some form of genetic defect," also called for increased support of research to identify genetically related disorders; development of better screening techniques, and better ways to provide genetic counseling services; improved care of those suffering from genetic disorders; and "exploration of the ethical and moral implications of genetic technology." To this end, increased private and public funding was urged to "develop facilities and train personnel to implement programs in genetic screening and counseling." . . .

The Status of Women

The report pointed out that women today "marry earlier, have smaller families earlier, and live longer than they did fifty years ago." With less and less of their lives spent in maternal functions, women more and more are beginning to work, seek higher education and "choose roles supplementary to or in place of motherhood." While this trend is likely to continue, and even intensify, with more women foregoing motherhood entirely, the Commission found that our society has "not yet fully accommodated these changes in our social, legal, and economic structures." The panel remarked that "it would seem good social policy to recognize and facilitate the trend toward smaller families by making it possible for women to choose attractive roles in place of or supplementary to motherhood." This change, the report stated, should not be sought on demographic grounds alone, but as a means of offering "a greater range of choice" so that men and women can "be free to develop as individuals rather than being molded to fit some sexual stereotype." The Commission stated that it would be "particularly helpful if marriage, childbearing, and childrearing could come to be viewed as more deliberate and serious commitments rather than as traditional, almost compulsory behavior."

The panel expressed doubt that jobs usually open to women, of low pay and status, have much effect in reducing fertility. It indicated, however, its belief that "attractive work may effectively compete with childbearing and have the effect of lowering fertility. . . ." The Commission also found "abundant evidence" that higher education is associated with smaller families, and urged that "institutional discrimination against women in education should be abolished."

Despite improvements in the legal status of women over the past century, the Commission stated that "equal rights and responsibilities are still denied women in our legal system." It urged that the proposed Equal Rights Amendment to the United States Constitution . . . be ratified by the states, and that "federal, state, and local governments undertake positive programs to ensure freedom from discrimination based on sex."

Child Care

The Commission found that the child-care arrangements made by working mothers—especially those with limited incomes—"are frequently inadequate." The Commission pointed to the "critical significance of the first three years of life for the emotional, and intellectual, as well as the physical, development of children." Adequate full-time developmental child-care programs, the Commission held, could tap the enormous learning potential of preschool children, and might also work to reduce fertility by offering women who want to work the opportunity to enter or re-enter the labor force much sooner than they would be able to otherwise. While such programs are expensive (the Commission cited one estimate of $20 billion per year for the "best kind" of program for the 18 million children from families with incomes under $7,000), the panel indicated that those who could afford to pay should do so, and union and industry programs should be expanded to help defray the costs. The Commission stated, however, that public funds would still be necessary to "stimulate innovative programs and research, and to subsidize services for lower-income families."

The Commission recommended that "public and private forces join together to assure that adequate child-care programs, including health, nutritional, and educational components, be available to families who wish to make use of them." It also urged continuing research and evaluation of the benefits and costs to children, parents and the public of various child-care arrangements.

The Commission found that "the demographic impact of adoption on the birthrate in the United States is minimal." Nevertheless, "the symbolic value of adoption as a mode of responsible parenthood ["adopt after two"] may come to outweigh its direct demographic impact." . . .

Immigration

The Commission pointed out that immigrants are now entering the United States at the rate of almost 400,000 a year, and that net immigration accounted for about 16 percent of total population growth between 1960 and 1970. If immigration were to continue at the present rate, and each immigrant family were to have an average of two children, then immigrants arriving between 1970 and the year 2000 and their descendants would account for almost a quarter of the population increase during that period. To achieve population stabilization and continue immigration at the present rate would require an average of 2.0 children per woman, rather than the 2.1 children needed for stabilization if there were no immigration. Such stabilization would occur at a later date and imply an eventual population about 8 percent larger than if there were no international migration.

Immigrants not only contribute to the growth of the population, but affect its distribution. Immigrants tend to prefer metropolitan areas and are concentrated in a few of the largest cities; two thirds of recent immigrants indicated their intention to settle in six states. The Commission urged that the flow of immigrants "be closely regulated until this country can provide adequate social and economic opportunities for all its present members, particularly those traditionally discriminated against because of race, ethnicity, or sex." Despite the problems associated with immigration, the Commission majority felt that the present level of immigration should be maintained because of "the compassionate nature of our immigration policy" and in recognition of "the contribution which immigrants have made and continue to make to our society." The Commission recommended, however, that "immigration levels not be increased and that immigration policy be reviewed periodically to reflect demographic conditions and considerations."

While urging a freeze on the level of *legal* immigration, the Commission called for a crackdown on *illegal* entry—which, it said, "exacerbated" many of our economic problems. The panel called for congressional legislation imposing "civil and criminal sanctions on employers of illegal border-crossers or aliens in an immigration status in which employment is not authorized."

Migration and Metropolitan Growth

With ever-increasing rapidity, the United States has been transformed in this century from a rural to a metropolitan society. At the beginning of the century, the Commission pointed out, six in ten Americans lived on farms or in villages. Today, nearly seven in ten live in cities of 50,000 or more, or in their suburbs; this proportion is likely, the Commission predicted, to grow to 85 percent before the century's end. Such metropolitan growth is the inevitable consequence, the report stated, of "the social and economic transformation of the United States . . . from an agrarian, to an industrial, and now to a service-oriented economy." Migration has been from low-income rural areas and from abroad to metropolitan areas, from one metropolitan area to another, and from central cities to suburbs. This pattern of growth has left in its wake such well-publicized problems as congestion in central cities, air and noise pollution, aesthetically unattractive suburban growth, and emergence of the "two societies"—poor blacks in the central cities, affluent whites in the suburbs.

"Population growth *is* metropolitan growth," the report

declared. The Commission pointed out, however, that while past migration to big-city areas lies at the root of present concentrations, natural increase is now "the dominant source of metropolitan growth" (three fourths of such growth over the past decade). The trend toward bigness of metropolitan areas cannot be checked substantially unless national population growth is slowed or stopped. Thus, the Commission reported, "the most effective long-term strategy for stabilizing local [metropolitan] growth is through national stabilization, not redistribution."

Nevertheless, the Commission held, there is a need to do something now about the problems brought about by population maldistribution; and there will still be problems of "congestion, pollution, and severe racial separation" in large metropolitan areas, even after stabilization is attained. The Commission called for "attenuating and simultaneously better accommodating" present trends in population distribution through a "dual strategy":

"encouraging the growth of selected urban centers in economically depressed regions," and

seeking "to enhance choices of living environments for all members of society. . . ."

Racial Polarization

The Commission deplored the increase in racial polarization which has occurred in the wake of metropolitan growth; it urged that "action be taken to increase freedom in choice of residential location through the elimination of current patterns of racial and economic segregation and their attendant injustices." This, the panel said, will require "vigorous and concerted steps" to promote bias-free housing within metropolitan areas and, specifically, assurance by federal and state governments that more suburban housing for low- and moderate-income families is built.

The Commission also called for more programs "to equip black and other deprived minorities for fuller participation in economic life," including coordinated programs of education, health, vocational development and job counseling.

While calling for a "long-run national policy of eliminating the ghetto," the Commission pointed to the "short-run need to make the ghetto a more satisfactory place to live." The panel urged that "actions be taken to reduce the dependence of local jurisdictions on locally collected property taxes" as one way of promoting a "more racially and economically integrated society." The Commission found that "given the heavy reliance of local jurisdictions on locally collected property taxes, the very structure of local government in metropolitan areas . . . provides incentives for people and activities to segregate themselves, which produces disparities between local resources, requirements, and levels of service, which in turn invite further segregation." The Commission called for a more "progressive" tax program, through which revenues are "raised on the basis of fiscal capacity and distributed on the basis of expenditure needs."

The Commission also advocated "restructuring of local governments" to reduce "overlapping jurisdictions with limited functions and the fragmentation of multipurpose jurisdictions. . . ." The Commission suggested that metropolitanwide government might be appropriate for some areas, and a "two-tier system" like Toronto's for others. . . .

The Economy and the Environment

Before making its recommendations, the Commission carefully investigated—and finally rejected—the opposing claims that, on the one hand, slowing population growth could hurt business or threaten workers' jobs, or, on the other hand, that we must take drastic measures to reach zero population growth quickly, lest we ravage all of our resources and irreversibly pollute the ecosphere.

On the economic side, the Commission stated that it had "looked for and . . . not found, any convincing economic argument for continued national population growth," in terms of the economy as a whole, of business or of "the welfare of the average person." Indeed, the Commission found, "the average person will be markedly better off" economically if we move toward replacement fertility than if families are larger.

As to ecological damage, the Commission found that population growth exacerbates but is not the "sole culprit" causing such problems. "To believe that it is," the report states, "is to confuse how things are done with how many people are doing them."

In the long run, the Commission said, the solutions to our ecological problems will require "conservation of water resources, restrictions on pollution emissions, limitations on fertilizers and pesticides, preservation of wilderness areas, and protection of animal life threatened by man." It will require "development of clean sources of energy production" such as nuclear fusion, and adequate "pricing of public facilities and common property resources . . . such as rivers and air." (The report remarked that "at present, most monetary incentives work the wrong way, inducing waste and pollution rather than the opposite.")

Gradually slowing population growth, the Commission pointed out, will not solve any of these ecological problems, but it will help us "buy time" to find sensible solutions. However, the Commission found no merit to "the emergency crisis response." Zero population growth could not be attained rapidly "without considerable disruption to society," including serious dislocations in employment, education and business as families' average childbearing was forced to shrink and expand, contract and enlarge again over several decades. In addition, the authoritarian means which would be necessary to attain these undesirable ends would probably be unenforceable, and certainly would be repugnant in a democratic society.

THE PRESIDENT'S REACTION [3]

President Nixon rejected major recommendations of his population commission . . . [early in May 1972], particularly those for abortion-on-request, unrestricted distribution of family planning services and supplying of contraceptive devices to minors.

"Such measures would do nothing to preserve and strengthen close family relationships," the President said in a statement.

He met afterwards with John D. Rockefeller III, chairman of the Commission on Population Growth and the American Future. The commission in March . . . [1972] completed a two-year study on population patterns.

It recommended that the nation's growth rate be reduced to zero—a point where births equal deaths—and to accomplish this that abortion laws be eased and that sex education and fertility control be made available to people of all ages.

"While I do not plan to comment extensively on the contents and recommendations of the report," the President's statement said, "I do feel it is important that the public know my views on some of the issues raised.

"In particular I want to reaffirm and reemphasize that I do not support unrestricted abortion policies—I consider abortion an unacceptable form of population control. In my judgment, unrestricted abortion policies would demean human life.

"I also want to make it clear that I do not support the unrestricted distribution of family planning services and devices to minors," Mr. Nixon said.

The commission had advocated abortion on request with the admonition that it not be considered the primary means of fertility control. The commission also recom-

[3] From article "Nixon Rejects Population Panel Advice," by Harry F. Rosenthal, Associated Press correspondent. Washington *Post*. p 1. My. 6, '72. © 1972 by The Washington Post. Reprinted by permission.

mended that families be encouraged to have only two children.

Addressing himself to this point Mr. Nixon said "I have a basic faith that the American people themselves will make sound judgments regarding family size and frequency of births, judgments that are conducive both to the public interest and to personal family goals.

"I believe in the right of married couples to make these judgments for themselves."

Thanks Commission

Despite an almost curt rejection of the major recommendation of the commission he himself appointed, the President expressed his thanks for its work and for the information assembled.

"The recommendations of the commission will be taken into account," he said, "as we formulate our growth and population research policies."

The President noted that many of the questions raised by the report cannot be answered purely on the basis of fact "but rather involve moral judgments about which reasonable men will disagree."

His statement noted that he does not plan to comment extensively on the fourteen-chapter report, which recommended among other things that states adopt laws to permit minors to receive contraceptive and prophylactic information and services, and payment by government and private health services for the full costs of all means of fertility control including voluntary sterilization.

Assailed by Catholic Group

When the first part of the report was made public March 16 [1972] the section on abortion was attacked by the United States Catholic Conference as leading "into an ideological valley of death."

But when the report had been issued in full a group of national Protestant and Jewish leaders urged the President to give it serious consideration despite his known opposition to abortion legislation.

"I would hope that abortion and sterilization would not be used as a red herring to draw attention away from the larger issues," said Bishop John Wesley Lord of the United Methodist Church.

In his statement Mr. Nixon noted that the extensive public discussion generated by the population commission report "clearly indicates the need to continue research in areas touching on population growth and distribution."

JUST HOW MANY IMMIGRANTS? [4]

People who are concerned about both immigration and population have lately become apprehensive about a calculation of the Commission on Population Growth and the American Future: Immigration to this country between 1960 and 1970 accounted for 16 percent of our annual population growth; it was responsible for 18 percent of our growth in 1971, and by 1972 it had jumped to 23 percent. In terms of the impact on total population in any single year, the effect seems slight: one immigrant arriving for every five hundred residents. But in terms of its impact on annual growth in numbers, it is considerable, amounting to nearly one out of every four persons added to the population each year. Any additional growth due to *illegal* immigration can only be guessed at. Net civilian immigration is not only alien immigration. The United States Census Bureau estimate of 400,000 immigrants a year includes not only alien immigrants but net arrivals of civilian citizens, Puerto Ricans, dependents and others. The actual number of alien immigrants admitted in 1971 was 370,478; and in 1972 was 384,685. . . . Records of US emigration are not kept.

[4] From article "Should We Pull Up the Gangplank?" by Leslie Aldridge Westoff, free-lance writer, coauthor of *From Now to Zero: Fertility, Contraception and Abortion in America.* New York *Times Magazine.* p 14-15+. S. 16, '73. © 1973 by The New York Times Company. Reprinted by permission.

The recent hysteria about population bombs, an ensuing movement to arrest population growth by stopping at two children per woman, the increasing concern about growing numbers of illegal aliens, the dismay of many developing countries which daily lose their young technicians in the continuing brain-drain process and a change in the kind of immigrants who wish to live in the United States have created a number of vital questions. Zero Population Growth, Inc., whose goal of reaching a stationary population seems to be on the way to being realized more quickly than it could have hoped for, decided at a . . . [1973] national meeting to focus its current energies on the last frontier of population growth, immigration. . . .

We are a "nation of immigrants." Thus, wouldn't it seem selfish to pull up the gangplank now that we're all aboard? To shut our ears to the echoes of our own past? Yet do we really any longer want the huddled, starving masses, the "wretched refuse" of other shores? We have, with missionary zeal, welcomed unfortunate people. . . . We have made immigration almost synonymous with liberty itself. But is it time to admit that immigration for us may no longer be a need but a dying historical symbol? Is the price of continuing it simply too high?

What exactly does immigration mean in terms of population numbers? In 1972 our fertility rate fell to . . . [2.03] births per woman, which is even below replacement—the 2.11 births per woman needed to replace one generation with the next and to keep the population ultimately at a stable number. . . .

We have been accepting nearly 400,000 legal immigrants annually into this country in recent years. The population commission observed that if *all* families, including immigrant families, just replaced themselves at the 2.1 average (contrary to the stereotype, immigrant women actually have lower fertility than native-born women) then between 1970 and the year 2000 the immigrants, plus all their descendants who are born here, will add up to about sixteen million people. This would be equal to the size of the entire crowded metropolitan area of New York City (which includes chunks of New Jersey and Connecticut). And that's a lot of extra humanity. . . . Furthermore, the Commission on Population Growth . . . emphasized that if we are to achieve stabilization and at the same time maintain the current volume of immigration, native-born women would have to continue to have fewer children, an average of slightly under 2.0. . . .

At this moment, the choice seems to be this: When the year 2000 arrives, do we want 250 million people (without immigration) or 268 million (with it)? If stabilization becomes a reality around the year 2040, . . . would we want 276 million people (without immigration) or 300 million (with it, and at a fertility rate *below* replacement)? *Or,* if fertility continued at replacement and current immigration continued, our population then would be 315 million and still growing.

What we must ask is whether our natural compassion for uniting families, the wish to offer a haven for refugees and the nostalgia for our melting-pot heritage justify adding 8 percent more people to our country. Whether it is worth having smaller families ourselves and reaching the point of no-more-growth at a later date.

Brain Drain

As a prosperous nation we have always been a country where doctors, researchers and technicians could find the kind of unexcelled training, intellectual stimulation, superb facilities and high salaries which simply weren't available elsewhere. For this reason, during the twenty years from 1946 to 1965, British and German professionals were soaked up by our expanding universities and great private research laboratories.

This trend continues. In 1960, 8 percent of our immigrants were professionals; by 1970, 12 percent. But because of the new immigration law passed in 1965, which abolished preferences for people of certain ethnic origins (northern European) and allowed people to enter from other ethnic backgrounds (southern European, African, Asian) who had not originally been represented in large numbers in our society, we now have a preponderance of professional immigrants from Asia and fewer from Europe. More than a quarter of all Asian immigrants and one third of all African immigrants are professional workers.

The brain drain from developed countries has now become the new brain drain from developing countries. This has produced a serious loss of scientific and professional personnel from lands which desperately need their trained people. . . .

For the United States, importing immigrant professionals is a cheap way of getting talent without investing in their training. It is estimated that we saved $4 billion by importing 100,000 scientists, engineers and physicians between 1949 and 1967. It has no doubt been more economical in the short run to import doctors than to build the thirty-five or more medical schools we need, each costing $20 million and $5 million a year to maintain.

There is little doubt that the foreign brains we've hired have helped put America on top in many ways—atomic science, space technology, medicine, engineering and so on. (Among American Nobel Prize winners, 41 percent were foreign-born, and one quarter of the National Academy of Science members were also born abroad.) Foreign-born composers, musicians, writers, painters have continuously enriched what has, with their help, come to be known as American culture. How much poorer we all would have been without Toscanini, Thomas Mann, an Einstein, a Wernher von Braun, a Stravinsky, a Kissinger, a Beatle—or the great French chef Henri Soulé. Many, however, were refugees from Nazi Germany, and welcoming aboard refugees (the Hungarians in the fifties, the Cubans in the sixties, and 1,200 Asians from Uganda in 1972), or giving refuge or a place to work to some of the great men and women of the world is another matter. But in the long run, the wholesale importing of average workers in the professions (Philippine schools are said to be mass-producing doctors for us, while Jamaica mass-produces nurses) can only be detrimental to everyone, the professionals, the sending nations and our own nation.

Though more and more professionals deluge our shores, most of our immigrants are nonprofessionals (30 percent), or those with no occupation (55 percent)—the housewives, children and students.

Though actual numbers of immigrants may not be a demographic crisis (unless you happen to feel that 8 percent more people than we ultimately might otherwise have constitutes a crisis), the economics of nonprofessional immigration presents something of a problem. . . .

Thus most immigrants head toward the large cities, close to relatives and employment. In cities like New York, Miami, Los Angeles, San Francisco, Chicago and Honolulu, thousands of new people add to the congestion, compete for housing, put additional pressure on the schools, medical services and welfare programs and flood the job market.

Illegal Aliens

Immigration has its other dilemmas. The most publicized of late is illegal immigration. It's a shocking fact that a small army of one, two, or possibly even three or four million (estimates vary this widely) illegal aliens live in this country, and that this number is increasing every year. Of course the Immigration and Naturalization Service finds some. The number of illegal aliens discovered annually is *greater* than the number of aliens admitted each year as legal residents. And this is merely the top of the iceberg.

In 1971, 420,000 deportable aliens were apprehended, which was 50,000 more than the number admitted legally. Of these, 76 percent entered illegally, most slipping over the two-thousand-mile Mexican border, and 24 percent had entered legally as crewmen, students, temporary laborers and visitors. They violated the conditions of their admission, and simply disappeared into our cities. In 1972, 506,000 illegals were located, 121,000 more than were legally admitted.

Eighty-five percent of the illegal aliens are Mexicans, whose motives are perfectly understandable. The economic imbalance between their country and ours is too great to be ignored. On one side of the line is poverty, on the other side is wealth. On one side the average wage *per day* is the equivalent of $1. On the other side it is $1 to $1.50 *per hour* in farm work, and $3.50 *per hour* in industry. On one side of the border is severe unemployment. The per capita income of Mexico is less than $150 a year. Our pull-factors are simply too great: jobs and money. . . .

Not only do illegal immigrants upset the low-income labor market, but they also make free use of our various assistance programs. In Texas, for example, there are 8,550 aliens receiving old age assistance, while immigration records show only 5,900 aliens over sixty-five living legally in Texas. Dr. Clifton Govan of the Colorado Department of Health estimates that from one sixth to one fifth of the state's health money is being spent on illegal aliens. . . . [And] there are said to be 500,000 illegal aliens living in New York City alone. . . .

Which Way to Go?

It is hard to turn our backs on people who are so desperate to come here. The Polish gypsies who tried three times on stolen German passports. The woman who hid a baby in her hand luggage. The thousands of others who want the kind of life that this country stands for.

Yet, there are many reasons for restricting immigration, as we are doing, and perhaps restricting it even more. In a national survey conducted by the Commission on Population Growth in 1971, some 50 percent of the people queried actually favored a reduction in immigration and 41 percent wanted it to remain the same. Since half the public appears to favor reduction, this may be something many of our lawmakers should consider seriously. . . .

Immigration, unfortunately, has its own built-in stimulus. We must remember that each time we let one person in from the Eastern Hemisphere as a permanent resident, his wife and unmarried sons and daughters will be able to be reunited with him, and if he becomes a United States citizen and is from either hemisphere, his parents, married sons and daughters, and unmarried brothers and sisters will be able to join him. So, in a sense, when we admit permanent resident aliens, we also admit their families, sooner or later.

What are some of the answers? How do we cope? Demographically, we can certainly survive with the additional population. . . .

Immigration could be used as a safety valve to help regulate our growth. There is nothing sacred about the figure 400,000. There is no reason in theory why we cannot enlarge or decrease this number as our birthrate shrinks and expands, encouraging or discouraging immigration depending upon the number of children American couples are having.

As far as the brain drain is concerned, if we persist in importing our talent rather than expanding our own facilities, we are not only enticing good people away from the developing countries which desperately need them, which can't be helping our foreign relations, but we also will be left with a continuing shortage of good doctors, engineers and scientists, find that we have compromised our standards of excellence and become increasingly dependent on what the rest of the world chooses to send us.

It might be appropriate to reduce our import of professionals until such time as those Americans who wish to pursue this kind of life have been able to realize their potential. This would also give the sending countries a chance to involve their technicians in the development of their own lands. . . .

It would probably be a blessing to both the United States and the rest of the world if, for the time being anyway, we turned off the brain drain to a mere trickle. . . .

Carl Pope, the Zero Population Growth lobbyist in Washington, believes that our present policy is irrational and should be reopened. He says we can't hope to absorb all those who want to come in, filling a few holes in the labor market is not a good enough reason to invite so many in, and we can reduce immigration substantially without interfering with our humanitarian goals. "Immigration is a sentimental symbol whose day is long past," says Pope. "We could take in 100,000 immigrants and still serve that symbol."

With the majority of the world still poor, . . . certainly the United States will continue to stand for the land of opportunity, and pressures to come here will persist. The pressures are often irresistible. But obviously, the fewer people we have, the easier it will be to solve our many problems: catch up on better housing; eliminate unemployment; help the poor, the blacks, realize their aspirations; provide better quality education, health care, welfare and more imaginative care for our senior citizens; conserve our natural resources; improve mass transportation . . . the whole laundry list of ailments we suffer.

ON POPULATION POLICY [5]

The Planned Parenthood Federation of America believes that the people of the United States must plan now for an early and orderly slowing of population growth and should work towards achieving a nation of stable size in an optimum environment. We recognize the great and increasing threat imposed upon the quality of national life by the many complex problems such as racism, poverty, hunger, malnutrition, unemployment, underemployment, lack of

[5] *Population Policy: Statement Adopted by Membership, 1972.* Planned Parenthood Federation of America. 810 Seventh Ave. New York 10019. '72.

saleable skills and ecological and environmental problems such as pollution of air, land, and water, destruction of irreplaceable natural resources and the erosion of ecological balances which are multiplied and intensified by continued and unchecked population growth. We recognize that the goal of a stable population to maintain a satisfactory quality of life must recognize the basic inequalities which presently exist for the poor of this country, whose environment and health care are already at an unacceptably low level. These conditions must be improved before we can expect the poor to share our concern for population stabilization.

Moreover, it must be recognized that a reduction in the population growth in itself will not solve these problems. We must apply our prestige and power to the elimination of such problems.

Nevertheless, every increase in population makes these social and economic problems more difficult to solve. Major changes in the attitudes and behavior of the American public are also essential to their solution.

We reject dictation of the number of children each family may have. There are, however, other means of helping to bring about the necessary reduction of the national rate of population growth:

1. developing and providing appropriate programs of information, education and training in family planning, family life, human sexuality and population, emphasizing the importance of these programs to the physical and mental health of men, women and children

2. offering comprehensive voluntary contraceptive services, sterilization services, and abortion to all

3. encouraging biomedical research to develop safer and more effective contraceptive technology, and encouraging socioeconomic and demographic research

4. removing all restrictive laws and policies pertaining in any way to the provision of voluntary contraceptive services, including those based on age, parental consent, mar-

ital status or economic criteria, and removing all laws and policies unreasonably restricting voluntary sterilization and abortion

As a part of our public information and education programs, the acceptance of various life styles should be stressed.

It is essential that the public be fully and accurately informed. Planned Parenthood can and will help to bring together existing knowledge regarding the threats to our environment and their relation to the growth rate and size of our population and provide information and education to the public on these and related questions.

In particular, we must explore all possible means to encourage people at all economic levels, including those in middle and upper income brackets, to have small families; taking note that the greater adverse impact on environment is made by the more affluent section of our society.

Finally, it must be repeated that in announcing this population policy, Planned Parenthood Federation of America must also commit its prestige and resources to assist in the elimination of the twin evils of poverty and institutional racism from our national life.

WHEN AND WHY ZERO GROWTH? [6]

The long term survival of the human species is dependent upon the establishment of an equilibrium between human demands and the carrying capacity of nature. The earth and its resources of land, air, water, and minerals are finite, and therefore there are limits to the cumulative demands which can be placed upon them. In addition, the earth and its resources and the users of those resources comprise a series of intricately complex ecological systems.

[6] *A Statement of the Goals of Zero Population Growth, Inc.* Zero Population Growth, Inc. 1346 Connecticut Ave. N.W. Washington, D.C. 20036. n.d. Reprinted by permission.

No demand or action can be considered in isolation; all things are interconnected.

Foremost among the pressures on the boundaries of finity and ecological balance is the strain of a growing human population now numbering in the billions. The number of human beings that the earth can support is a function of the per capita demands of those individuals. It is preferable to support a smaller number of human beings at an equitable and sufficient standard of living than a greater number at a lesser level.

Zero Population Growth, Inc. (ZPG) concerns itself primarily with the United States, but these principles are universal.

ZPG has adopted a limited number of broad goals to guide its activities:

1. ZPG believes that the present population of the United States exceeds the optimum level for the continued well-being of its citizens. ZPG therefore advocates the achievement, by voluntary means, of an end to US population growth by 1990, and a reduction in US population size thereafter. Among the conditions necessary to achieve this goal, ZPG stresses: freedom of access for every person to all means of voluntary birth control; a major research effort to develop safer and more effective means of birth control; complete equality of opportunity for all women and men; and removal of all legal and societal pronatalist pressures. The population size should stabilize at a substantially reduced level which will maximize diversity, freedom of choice, and the quality of life for all.

2. ZPG believes that land is a resource too important to human survival to be subjected to misuse. Ecological land use planning is essential in determining the appropriate patterns of distribution of people on the land, and of migration between states and regions. Thoughtful land use planning at all levels of government is necessary to assure the long-range stewardship of the land and well-being of mankind.

3. ZPG believes that human activities are causing the rapid depletion of the world's available stock of mineral resources. Simultaneously those activities are resulting in increased pollution of land, air and water resources. ZPG therefore recommends (1) reduction in the rate of growth and eventual stabilization of United States consumption of nonrenewable resources; and (2) rapid stabilization of total national energy consumption at least until environmentally sound sources are developed.

ZPG recognizes that none of its goals can be justified unless concurrently with their achievement adequate levels of income, health care, and educational opportunity are assured to all persons.

ZPG: WHAT AND HOW? [7]

When in 1967 "zero population growth" was first mentioned as a goal of population policy, it was not itself defended or discussed; only the means of reaching it were considered. Since that time, with ZPG becoming the name for a movement, a lively debate has ensued over the goal as well as the means. In what follows, I shall first consider some of the main developments in the debate, then search for what lies behind the debate, hoping to illuminate the nature of population policy.

The question at issue when ZPG was introduced was whether the population policies then current were effective or ineffective. To answer that question, one obviously needed to know what goal the policies were trying to achieve. A search of the literature of the population movement revealed no clear statement of the goal. "Population control" could not be considered a goal, because it did not specify "control to what end." However, since population

[7] From "Zero Population Growth: The Goal and the Means," by Kingsley Davis, director of international population and urban research, University of California at Berkeley. *Daedalus.* 102:15-29. Fall '73. Reprinted by permission of *Daedalus,* Journal of the American Academy of Arts and Sciences, Boston, Mass. Fall 1973, *The No-Growth Society.*

control was frequently justified in the policy literature by graphic accounts of the dangers of population increase—dangers seldom specific for given rates of increase but ascribed to any continued exponential rate—I drew the conclusion that the implied aim was no population growth at all. I therefore undertook to determine whether the population measures being pursued or advocated in official circles were likely to achieve ZPG. Although a prominent fellow demographer described me as having "vigorously endorsed" the goal of ZPG, the question was simply, *if* ZPG is the goal, will the measures being adopted succeed or fail? The answer was independent of whether I or anyone else actually held that aim, but, as subsequent debate proved, ZPG or even NPG (negative population growth) was indeed a common aspiration among people concerned about population growth.

My conclusion was that measures then current did not provide population control for any collective purpose, least of all for population stability. Limited to "family planning" and hence to couple control, about all they could accomplish would be to help countries approaching a modern condition reach *an industrial level* of fertility, a level they would soon reach anyway. An industrial level, however, is far above ZPG. Between 1960 and 1970, for example, the fifty industrial countries of the world increased their population by 14 percent, a rate that would double it in less than fifty years. As a class these countries had a more rapid increase after World War II than the underdeveloped countries ever had before that.

For ZPG as a goal, it was unfortunate that the concept first arose in the context of a critique of family planning as the exclusive approach to population policy. The powerful interests vested in this approach reacted by attacking not only the idea that other means than family planning might be necessary, but also the goal of ZPG itself. Spokesmen for the population programs of foundations, international agencies, and government bureaus—all committed to the

assumption that the population problem is due to unwanted births (unwanted, that is, by the people who have
them) and that therefore the solution is to provide massive
contraceptive services—felt that their leadership had been
challenged. Accused either of not pursuing a goal that many
of their ardent supporters had assumed they were pursuing
and which their own arguments seemed to imply, or else of
using means incapable of reaching that goal, they had
either to deny the goal or to affirm the adequacy of the
means. Actually, they began by doing both but later yielded
ground, especially with reference to the goal. Let us examine the arguments and counterarguments.

ZPG as a Goal

To declare that ZPG was not the goal of existing population programs was dangerous. Yet soon after the ZPG concept appeared, three leaders of the population movement
not only made this declaration but went further to say
that the family-planning program, at least in the United
States, is not for population limitation at all. "The federal
program [of family planning] has been advanced," they
said, "not for population control, but to improve health
and reduce the impact of poverty and deprivation." Others
were less hasty. They did not directly repudiate ZPG as a
goal but painted its advocates as naive, unrealistic, or authoritarian. For instance, the uncertain *timing* of ZPG was
used as a basis for criticism. By interpreting ZPG advocates
as demanding ZPG immediately, critics could accuse them
of being enthusiasts, ignorant of the science of demography,
who were unwittingly threatening Americans with a child
embargo. On the other hand, by interpreting them as wanting ZPG only sometime in the indefinite future, critics
could say that they were merely recommending the inevitable. These points are worth examining.

Immediate ZPG would certainly require a drastic reduction in fertility. Since existing societies have had more
births than deaths, their age structure is younger and more

favorable to future births than it would otherwise be. To compensate for this fact, if instant ZPG were to be attained, each current young woman would have to reduce her fertility, on the average, below her own replacement. This prospect was described in frightening terms:

Dr. [Tomas] Frejka warns that to achieve zero population growth immediately, it would be necessary for each family to limit itself to one child only for the next 20 years or so, with two-child families not permissible until after the year 2000. (*Family Planning Perspectives*, October 1970)

The United States Population Commission said that the sudden drop in reproduction would create a regrettable cyclical fluctuation in fertility.

This [ZPG] would not be possible without considerable disruption to society. . . . In a few years, there would be only half as many children as there are now. This would have disruptive effects on the school system and subsequently on the number of persons entering the labor force. . . . The overall effect would be that of an accordion-like continuous expansion and contraction. (*Population Studies*, November 1968)

Actually, Frejka found that, with migration excluded, a US population fixed from 1965 would require age-specific birthrates [birthrates of women in specific age groups] during the next twenty years which, if experienced by each woman during her reproductive life, would yield an average of 1.2 children per woman. However, not all women bear children. Among white women aged thirty-five to thirty-nine in the United States in 1960, some 15.5 percent had either never married or never borne a child. So, in Frejka's fixed population, each woman who *did* have a child could bear, on the average, 1.4 children—a mean that could be reached if 60 percent had one child and 40 percent had two. Put in these terms, instantaneous ZPG does not sound so frightening. As for "disruption to society," the resulting fluctuation in school-age children would be less than that actually experienced in the past. During the twenty years from 1950 to 1970 the number of children aged five to nineteen in continental United States shot up from 34.9 million to 59.5 million, a 70 percent increase. In Frejka's hypothetical calculations of ZPG beginning in 1965, the most drastic change in children of this age would be that of the twenty-five-year period from 1965 to 1990, when the number would fall by 41.5 percent.

In trying to discredit immediate ZPG, the Population Establishment was arguing against a straw man, because ZPGers, scarcely so literal-minded, would have been happy to see ZPG achieved within their lifetime. But not content with hitting them over the head for presumably wanting ZPG instantaneously, the Establishment buffeted them for the opposite as well, for supposedly wanting it in the indefinite future. "Zero growth," said [Dr. Frank W.] Notestein [demographer], "is . . . not simply a desirable goal; it is the only possibility in a finite world. One cannot object to people who favor the inevitable." The answer to this was given by Judith Blake:

By this reasoning, the human effort to control the time and manner of all sorts of inevitabilities—the effort expended on postponing death, maintaining houses, saving money—is all pointless. The spokesmen for ZPG do not argue that a stationary world population will never come about without ZPG policy, but rather that, without directed effort, zero growth will occur only after human numbers have greatly increased over present levels, and perhaps then by the mechanism of high mortality instead of fertility control. (*Population Index*, October-December, 1970)

. . . Apart from cavils about the timing of ZPG, there were two objections to a nongrowing population regardless of when it came about: that it would interfere with economic development and that it would produce a high proportion of aged persons. These arguments, both old, are worth examining.

The economic argument holds that some population growth is a good thing because it provides economies of scale, promotes a bullish investment psychology, and provides openings for the young; but, as the economist Stephen Enke pointed out, "the more slowly population grows the more capital can be accumulated per member of the labor force," and "only those who own something valuable and scarce can count on larger real incomes as a result of population growth." His simulation models for the United States show that a net reproduction rate of unity [when each woman has, on an average, one child] from 1975 on would yield a higher per capita GNP than either of two higher growth trends.

One has only to look at history to see that slow population growth does not mean economic stagnation nor does fast growth mean prosperity. Between 1890 and 1940 Ireland's population *declined* by 16 percent, yet during that period, according to figures compiled by Colin Clark, the real product per manhour rose by 99 percent, whereas in Great Britain, whose population grew by 42 percent, the improvement in product was only 62 percent. France, whose population rose more slowly than Britain's, had a rate of rise in real product nearly three times that of Britain. Sweden had such a low fertility that its cohorts born after 1885 were not replacing themselves, yet after that time it had what is probably the most rapid economic rise and is now the richest country in Europe. If human productivity is a function of resources and technology, and if resources are limited (as they indubitably are), the way to get a higher product—once population has gone beyond the point of providing adequate specialization—is to advance technology and decrease population. . . .

The other objection—that ZPG means an aged population—was voiced as follows in 1968:

A stationary population with an expectation of life of seventy years has as many people over sixty as under fifteen. . . . A society with such an age structure is not likely to be receptive to change, and indeed would have a strong tendency towards nostalgia and conservatism.

Actually, there are three questions involved here. First, since "life expectancy" is an average, can the age distribution vary independently of that average? The answer is yes, because it is affected by the skew in deaths by age. Suppose, for example, that in a stationary population everybody died at exactly age 70. The proportion of the population under age fifteen would be 21.4 percent, and over sixty, 14.3 percent. [Second,] even assuming a probable distribution of deaths by age, would the age structure of a ZPG population be highly abnormal? . . . [If] ZPG starts immediately and . . . is reached sometime between 1995 and 2000, . . . not only . . . [would] the proportion aged sixty-five plus [be] considerably less than that found in West Berlin now and close to that found in Sweden, but the distribution . . . [would be] especially favorable to economic production because of the high proportion of people in the productive ages. Third, would the age distribution of a ZPG population "disrupt the normal workings of the society"? Again no. There seems to be no correlation between the age structure and political outlook. The age distribution of the USSR is very similar to that of the USA; socialist Sweden has an older age structure than Falangist Spain. Some of the wildest political schemes ever known have been advocated by lobbies of the elderly and some of the most atavistic movements (such as the Nazi movement in Germany) were manned by dogmatic youth. . . . The South African white population is much younger than that of Sweden or West Berlin, but we do not associate South Africans with progressive liberalism.

The big difference in age structure is not between one industrial country and another, with or without ZPG, but between industrial and nonindustrial countries. This . . . [can be] demonstrated . . . by comparing Honduras with . . . [industrialized] countries. In Honduras only 40 percent of the population is in the productive ages [twenty to sixty-four] compared to 58 percent in Sweden and 57 percent in

West Berlin. ZPG would place the highest proportion in the productive ages.

What has happened, then, to ZPG as a goal? In the end the Establishment, in the form of the United States Population Commission, professed ZPG as its goal, but without using the term or endorsing its immediate attainment:

Recognizing that our population cannot grow indefinitely, and appreciating the advantages of moving now toward the stabilization of population, the Commission recommends that the nation welcome and plan for a stabilized population.

This was a remarkable victory for the ZPG movement in six years, but of course it did not mean benign consensus. Much goal conflict remained hidden, to emerge only when means were considered.

The Means to ZPG

If ZPG were the supreme aim, *any* means would be justified. By common consent, however, raising the death rate is excluded; also, reducing immigration is played down. This leaves fertility reduction as the main avenue. (In the past, had population growth been feared above all else, deaths would never have been reduced below births.) If then, the means is birth limitation, why not take measures to reduce births? Why not simply limit each couple to two births, with sufficient penalties to discourage three?

The response of the Population Establishment is that this would be "compulsion." Although plenty of compulsion has been used to lower death rates, it is not to be used to lower birthrates. On the contrary, the right of couples to have the number of children they want has been declared by policy leaders to be "a fundamental human right."

What lies behind this response? When the aim is game protection, the conservationists do not proclaim each hunter's right to shoot as much game as he wants. When the goal is clean air, the authorities do not assert each person's right to put as many pollutants into the air as he pleases.

Why, to achieve birth limitation, is it efficient to give each woman the right to have as many children as she wants?

The answer is that the problem is wrongly diagnosed—like attributing anemia to excess blood and prescribing bloodletting as the remedy. The assumption behind the "freedom-to-choose" emphasis in population policy is that the population problem is a function of unwanted births and therefore, if women have the means to limit births, the population problem will be solved.

But why make such a dubious assumption? The key lies in our unstated background. Our mores were formed when societies could survive only with a birthrate thrice that required by a modern death rate. Built into the social order, therefore, are values, norms, and incentives that motivate people to bear and rear children. These cultural and institutional inheritances form the premises of our thinking. Respected leaders of society are not about to disavow them, nor is the general public likely to do so. Accordingly, what is strategically required, if one wants to be a population policy leader, is a formula that appears to reduce reproduction without offending the mores that support it. The formula is to interpret the social problem as an individual one and the solution as a technological matter. Thus "fertility control" becomes control by the woman, not by society; and the means becomes a medically approved contraceptive. By this formula, population policy embraces research on the physiology of reproduction (to find better contraceptives), diffusion of contraceptive services (to get the devices to the women), and propaganda about the use of contraceptives and about the right of each woman to have as many children as she wants. The only traditional attitude affronted by this formula is the belief that God forbids birth control, as indeed he did in most religions, for good reasons. This belief, however, is not directly attacked by the family planners, but rather flanked by an ingenious concretizing of God's will. Each woman, say the family planners, should be free to choose a method "consonant with her religious beliefs." Since God did not specifically forbid the contraceptive pill or the plastic IUD [intrauterine device], these should be acceptable; but if they are not, some other method must be.

The respectability of this approach to population policy is reinforced not only by its appeal to health and medical authority and its link with science (reproductive physiology) but also by its preoccupation with parenthood and children. "Family planning" and "planned parenthood" implicitly feature the family. Nearly every family-planning booklet depicts on the front two radiantly happy offspring, and on the inside implies that every woman's main concern is her children, a concern that alone justifies her limiting their number.

Any other means than family planning tends to be characterized as "unacceptable" and/or "compulsory." The Committee on Population of the Academy [American Academy of Arts and Sciences], for example, declared in *Science* (February 1968) that "many of his [Davis'] arguments are unlikely to be approved. . . ." This objection is unassailable. Virtually all proposed social changes are initially unacceptable, or else they would not need to be proposed. If ZPG is the goal, "existing values" are not a help but a hindrance, for they are pronatalist [encourage the bearing of children] in character, and measures entirely conforming to them will not bring ZPG. For that reason measures to stop population growth cannot be found which can be guaranteed in advance to be acceptable. They have to *win* acceptance, and this can be done only if the benefits of ZPG are demonstrated and the encouragements to reproduction in the old system exposed. In that case the public will accept modification of the received incentive system, although it will never tolerate throwing away the entire institutional order insofar as family and children are concerned. In calling for approval in advance, the family-planning movement confuses the issues. The question of whether a policy, *if adopted,* would succeed is different from the question of whether, *if proposed,* it would be accepted. Clarity requires that the two questions be kept analytically distinct; in practice, demonstration that a policy would or would not be effective may influence its acceptability. My judgment is that, in the absence of clear analysis, family planning was acceptable as population policy precisely because it conformed to social sentiments and had not been challenged. . . .

If it is true that the Population Establishment has espoused ZPG but has clung to family planning (broadened to include abortion, sterilization, and teenage services and sex education) as the means for reaching it, there are two questions: Have demographic events proved the Establishment to be right? If they have not, what additional means may be necessary?

Recent Population Trends and Population Policy

In the last few years spectacular declines in birthrates have given heart to the leaders of the population movement. In the United States, for example, the births per one thousand women aged fifteen to forty-four reached a peak in 1957, then fell until, in 1972, the rate was only 60 percent of the 1957 figure. This has led to widespread elation that our fertility has reached, or fallen slightly below, a replacement rate. "Couples are now averaging 2.04 children per family," said the Population Crisis Committee in March 1973, "which is below the 2.11 child replacement rate." However, the Committee knew that this meant zero growth only in the . . . [longrun], for it added: "If this rate continues for some seventy years, US population would stabilize or even decline slightly." There is no likelihood whatever that a fertility rate found in one year will continue for seventy years, and there is no way to find out what it will in fact do. To know how many children "couples are averaging," one would have to follow couples to the end of their reproductive period, which would take too long. A way to get some indication in advance is to ask young peo-

ple how many children they intend to have. This was done
. . . by the Census Bureau in June 1972. The expectations,
the lowest on record, led the Bureau to the conclusion that
women eighteen to twenty-four years old in 1972 might
"complete their childbearing with an average of about 2.1
births per woman [which] approximates 'replacement level
fertility.'" The only trouble is that since expectations have
changed in the past, they may change in the future. Indeed,
. . . young people may have been unduly influenced by the
nihilistic mood of the period from 1964 to 1972; . . . [in the
future they] may be more favorable to the family. This
possibility is suggested by actual fertility trends.

In the decline of fertility in the United States after 1957,
. . . [a low] *monthly* rate was reached in July of 1972, when
the seasonally adjusted general fertility rate (births per one
thousand women aged fifteen to forty-four was 68.2. . . .
[Since then] the rate has been slightly higher. Such a change
of direction is what one would expect, because in all industrial countries the birthrate since 1920 has exhibited a
strongly cyclical character. Also, in the twenty-one of these
countries for which recent data are available, the trend in
the crude birthrate between 1970 and 1971 was, on the
average, upward.

The drop in the American birthrate was particularly
sharp between 1970 and 1972, when the new state abortion
laws came into effect. Liberal abortion laws permit women
who become pregnant through carelessness . . . or desire to
get married an opportunity to remedy their mistake. This
effect is limited, however, and of itself cannot keep exerting
a downward pressure on fertility. The main effect of the
new abortion laws was probably to postpone by two or
three years the cyclical rise in American fertility.

Not only are industrial countries at present far from a
zero rate of natural increase, but they are receiving large
numbers of migrants from the less developed countries.
Thus in the United States in 1972, when the birthrate was
at its lowest ebb, the population increased by 1.628 million

people, of whom 1.29 million derived from more births than deaths and 338,000 from net migration. As long as the less developed two thirds of the world continues to increase its population at a rapid rate, the pressure on the developed third to receive massive immigration will be enormous. Are official policies likely to bring ZPG in the latter countries?

The spectacular decline of birthrates in many less developed countries is frequently taken as evidence of successful population policy. For example, in eight countries (Ceylon [Sri Lanka], Chile, Costa Rica, Egypt, Fiji, Jamaica, Taiwan, and Trinidad), between 1960 and 1970, the crude birthrate fell, on the average, by 27 percent. However, as is usual in citing such statistics, these countries were selected because in general their data are reasonably reliable, which means that on the whole they are more advanced than most underdeveloped countries. It is precisely in such countries—those on the verge of becoming urban-industrial —that the fastest declines in fertility have occurred. This suggests that the declines are being caused by changing social and economic conditions rather than by family-planning policy. In fact, it seems to make little difference whether the country has a major family-planning program or not, or, if it does have one, when it began. In Taiwan, where there is a much publicized quasi-official family-planning program, the birthrate dropped by 29 percent between 1960 and 1970, but in Trinidad, where there is no such program, the birthrate fell from almost exactly the same level by 38 percent. Furthermore, in Taiwan the family-planning program did not get started until 1964, before which time the drop in fertility was already rapid. It is hard to escape the conclusion that official programs of the sort being adopted around the world have little to do with the trend of birthrates. To be sure, most of the decline is due to the use of contraception, abortion, and sterilization, but the public, if it wishes to limit births, will find a way to get the means; if it does not wish to limit births, no official program for providing services will lead it to do so.

If family-planning policies, even when broadened somewhat as they have been in the last few years, are not likely to bring about ZPG, then additional and more drastic measures may be required. Before hastening to imagine such measures, however, we might first make an attempt to rethink the problem.

The Nature of Population Policy

The hypothesis must be entertained that the goal of population policy is too weak—that if the goal were strong enough, the means would be found. If this is so, the reason may be that population growth does not have serious consequences, or that people are ignorant of those consequences, or that to eliminate population growth would require too much sacrifice of other things. My hunch is that the last two explanations are the most likely.

From the standpoint of being solved, the population problem has three strikes against it. First, it refers to a condition of the community at large. It is not a personal disaster like drug addiction or bankruptcy; on the contrary, it is an outgrowth of personal satisfaction. Second, it is a problem that evolves slowly and therefore never reaches a sudden crisis. Unlike war, famine, fuel shortage, or political scandal, it does not appear at a particular moment and demand instant action. Third, it is not a problem "out there" in the external world, like crop disease or soil deficiency, to be dealt with by science and technology. The overabundant population is composed of people. When people themselves are the problem, the solution is always difficult, because subject and object are one and the same.

If the population problem were easily soluble, it would have been solved a century ago. By 1850 anyone could see that the revolution in productive technology enabled fewer people to manage more resources. Instead of utilizing this fact and limiting population growth, thereby providing themselves with a utopian level of living with little effort, the Europeans used it overwhelmingly to support more people. Europe became the world's most densely settled continent and, in turn, sent out migrants to overrun whole new continents. As other peoples came into contact with modern technology, they too eventually multiplied instead of decreasing their numbers. As a result, the human species is now in the preposterous situation of using an extremely advanced technology to maintain nearly four billion people at a low average level of living while stripping the world of its resources, contaminating its water, soil, and air, and driving most other species into extinction, parasitism, or domestication.

It is now too late to "solve" the world's population problem. Much that has been destroyed or wasted can never be restored. To reach without mass slaughter the small population compatible with a scientific technology will require centuries of negative population growth. What is being discussed now is not a solution but an amelioration. Standing in the way even of amelioration, however, are the same myths, interests, and conflicts that prevented a solution in the first place. Man has been shrewd enough to figure out the process of evolution but not wise enough to master it. The process has two principles: first, the world belongs to whatever animal can breed faster than it dies; and second, the world never belongs very long to one animal. The human race could escape being a victim of evolution if it were willing to forgo being its darling, but this it has not done, at least up to the present.

Recent history suggests, however, that ZPG is gaining strength as a goal. If so, what are the reasons? Whatever they are, they are to a large extent feedbacks from the unplanned and undesired human multiplication since World War II—1.5 billion people added to the population in twenty-eight years. This has led to disenchantment with growth in general and with economic growth in particular as a goal of human endeavor, because the double multiplier—more people times more goods per person—is obviously stripping the world of its metals and fossil fuels faster than either multiplier alone would do, and also making the world more unpleasant and inconvenient as a place to live. As normally measured, per capita income is simply an index of activity entering the exchange system. Up to a point, it bears some relation to satisfaction, but as population density and technological complexity increase, an ever larger proportion of human exchange activity is devoted simply to escaping the consequences of a high level of exchange activity. Sensing this, people are coming to view population growth as a problem, not because it restrains economic activity but because it makes its effects worse. If there were only 25 million Americans, they would not have to put antismog devices on their cars. Their "level of living" would therefore be lower, because this "economic activity" (making and installing antismog devices) would not be added to the economy.

The onus of proof is shifting from those who want ZPG or NPG [Negative Population Growth] to those who do not. Formerly, population stability had to be justified by citing *future* calamities that would result from continued population growth. Now, with a more sophisticated view, it is taken for granted that the calamities are not distant but here and now. Also, it was once considered inhuman to object to people; now the sheer frustration of dealing with people is readily acknowledged. The effort to escape the crush—to escape the city in the suburbs, to escape the suburbs in a second home in the country, to escape vacationers in the countryside—all attest the desire of people to escape from people. Formerly, too, a nongrowing population was regarded as abnormal; now, with wider knowledge of demographic history, it is realized that ZPG is normal and that the growth in the last two centuries is abnormal. The only thing abnormal about ZPG as now proposed is that it would be achieved with low rather than with high birth and death rates, which is why its detractors stress the small families, the older age structure, and the alleged social and economic difficulties that would result from those features.

How to Attain ZPG

The unconscious assumption that solving the population problem is a technological matter has a curious consequence for the demographer. He is constantly told, "Tell us what can be done about population," with the implication that if he cannot come up with a satisfactory answer, he is a failure. It is of no importance that the demographer has already made suggestions. These are brushed aside as not being practical. The demand is for "a solution that will work." What is being demanded is some mysterious "key" to population limitation, which can unlock the door painlessly and quickly. If only enough money is put into research, the thinking goes, if only the right disciplines are brought to bear, the solution will be "discovered."

The truth is that there is no mystery about population control. There is no special "technique" required, because the technological part is simple. If people want to control population, it can be done with knowledge already available. As with other social problems, the solution is easy as long as one pays no attention to what must be given up. For instance, a nation seeking ZPG could shut off immigration and permit each couple a maximum of two children, with possible state license for a third. Accidental pregnancies beyond the limit would be interrupted by abortion. If a third child were born without license, or a fourth, the mother would be sterilized and the child given to a sterile couple. But anyone enticed into making such a suggestion risks being ostracized as a political or moral leper, a danger to society. He is accused of wanting to take people's freedom away from them and institute a Draconian dictatorship over private lives. Obviously, then, reproductive freedom still takes priority over population control. This makes a solution of the population problem impos-

sible because, by definition, population control and reproductive freedom are incompatible.

Why, however, are people so concerned with freedom
in connection with reproduction? Freedom has always been
denied to murderers, rapists, and armed thieves. If having
too many children were considered as great a crime against
humanity as murder, rape, and thievery, we would have no
qualms about "taking freedom away." Indeed, it would be
defined the other way around: a person having four or
more children would be regarded as violating the freedom
of those other citizens who must help pay for rearing, educating, and feeding the excess children. The reason why
reproductive freedom is still regarded as "a basic human
right" regardless of circumstances is of course that it accords
with traditional sentiments and established institutions.
These, it will be recalled, are pronatalist. Reproductive
freedom can be construed as antinatalist only to the degree
that it undermines the built-in profertility compulsions of
the old system, which, however, as I have noted, are not or-
dinarily felt to be compulsions until attention is called to
them.

Thus the "population problem" is not a technological
problem. It is not something the definition of which is universally agreed upon and the solution to which awaits only
the discovery of an effective means. It is not like yellow
fever or wheat rust. It is a social problem in the sense that
it involves a conflict of wants. People want families and
children. If they did not want families and children, it
would be technologically easy to satisfy them. But they do
want families and children. That being the case, they are
not whole hearted about population control. They do not
want runaway population growth either, but they want to
avoid it painlessly. They want a solution that leaves them
their freedom to have five children if they wish. In short,
they want a miracle.

PEOPLE AND THE ENVIRONMENT [8]

In its examination of the impact of the US population on resources, . . . the Commission on Population Growth and the American Future may have left the most important stones unturned. For the Commission assumed, in concluding that the resource needs of an expanding US population can be met without great difficulty, that we would continue to have access to rich foreign deposits of fuels and minerals. Whether this actually will (or even should) be so hinges on deep and unresolved questions. How serious will the tensions be between the United States and increasingly prosperous but resource-poor Japan and Europe, as we compete for the world's remaining rich ores? Will the US balance of payments be able to bear the bill? Does the rate at which the United States extracts high-grade raw materials from less developed countries today compromise the ability of those countries to develop tomorrow, when only low-grade ores remain? Can the prosperity gap between the rich and poor nations of the world be narrowed at a meaningful rate without drastic modification of present patterns of resource consumption?

It is well known that the United States accounts for roughly one third of the world's annual consumption of energy, and a similar fraction of the consumption of most industrial metals. The combination of the United States, the Soviet Union, Europe, Japan and Australia accounts for 85 percent or more of the world's consumption of energy, steel, and tin. The United States in 1970 was importing 100 percent of its chromium, 94 percent of its manganese, almost 70 percent of its nickel and tin, and 22 percent of its petroleum. It has also been calculated, as a measure of the prosperity gap, that to supply the present world

[8] From "Population and the American Predicament: The Case Against Complacency," by John P. Holdren, assistant professor of energy and resources, University of California at Berkeley. *Daedalus.* 102:35-8. Fall '73. Reprinted by permission of *Daedalus,* Journal of the American Academy of Arts and Sciences, Boston, Mass. Fall 1973, *The No-Growth Society.*

population with the average per capita "standing crop" of industrial metals characteristic of the ten richest nations would require more than sixty years' world production of these metals at the 1970 rate. (Of course, the world population is growing, and, under existing patterns, the vast bulk of the extracted materials will go not to establish the underpinnings of prosperity in the poor countries but to support wasteful practices and further industrial growth in the rich ones.) Such figures need little elaboration. They suggest that even moderate population growth in rich countries exerts a disproportionate pressure on global resource flows, all else being equal, and that rapid progress toward developing the poor countries may be possible only if resource consumption is stabilized in the rich ones. Stabilized consumption, of course, is unlikely unless population size has also been stabilized.

That the United States is in for a period of relative resource scarcity and balance-of-payment problems is hard to doubt, regardless of how one views the likelihood of a major diversion of resource consumption from rich countries to poor ones. The present worsening petroleum situation is illustrating this problem all too vividly. So far, it is also leaving room for question as to whether the price mechanism can handle such difficulties smoothly (although, in fairness, it may be argued that mismanagement and inept regulation have not given the price mechanism a chance). In any case, the growing "energy crisis" has led to a predictable clamor for relaxation of environmental standards that have impeded development of new supplies. Curiously, the role that continued population growth will play in pushing up demand in an already precarious situation has not received as much attention.

The Role of Population

The reason for the widespread neglect of the population factor in the energy situation—and most other problems related to resources and environment—is that many ob-

servers regard such problems as primarily the result of
faulty technologies and high rates of growth of consumption per capita rather than of population size or growth
rate. This view can only arise from a failure to comprehend
the implications of the multiplicative relationships that actually prevail. Essentially, total consumption equals population times consumption per capita; total pollution equals
total consumption times pollution per unit of consumption.
Perhaps the basic point is that it is not meaningful to try
to divide the "responsibility" for a given level of total consumption (or pollution) between population size and consumption (or pollution) per person. Such a procedure is
analogous to trying to apportion the responsibility for the
area of a rectangle between the lengths of the two sides. The
property of interest, whether geometric area or population
pressure, resides inextricably in the combined action of the
contributing factors.

One can, on the other hand, distinguish among the relative contributions made by the rates of change of the various contributing factors to the rate of change of the total.
Even in this strictly arithmetical exercise, however, it is
easy to be misled, particularly when percentages are used.
Consider the true statement, "Total energy consumption
in the United States increased 1100 percent (twelvefold) between 1880 and 1966, while population increased 300 percent (fourfold)." On a quick reading, one might infer from
this statement that population growth was not the major
contributing factor. Actually, the increase in energy consumption per capita in this period was only 200 percent
(threefold); the twelvefold increase in total energy use is
the product, not the sum, of the fourfold increase in population and the threefold increase in use per person.

That simultaneously growing multiplicative factors yield
a disproportionately growing product leads to even more
startling numbers when three factors are considered rather
than two. For example, an observed increase of 415 percent
in emissions of automotive lead in the United States be-

tween 1946 and 1967 proves to have been generated by a 41 percent increase in population, a 100 percent increase in vehicle-miles per person, and an 83 percent increase in emissions per vehicle mile ($1.41 \times 2.00 \times 1.83 = 5.15$). The dramatic increase in total impact arose from rather moderate but simultaneous increases in the contributing factors; no factor was unimportant. Performing the same kinds of calculations on a variety of statistics shows, for the post-World War II period in the United States, that in strictly numerical terms the role of population growth in contributing to pressures on resources and environment has been substantial but not dominant. Neither, however, has either of the other major contributors to these pressures—rising affluence and technological change—been consistently dominant.

Does the conclusion that population is a significant factor in the United States still hold in the 1970s, with population growing at 1 percent per year while per capita consumption of many kinds grows at 4 percent? In a word, yes. It should be obvious that the impact of rapid growth of consumption per capita is greater in a large population than in a small one, and, correspondingly, that the *absolute* impact of an increment in population is increased by rapid growth of the per capita consumption factor that the population multiplies. . . . It is equally clear that the absolute significance of a fixed percentage increment of population goes up with the size of the base to which that increment is added—1 percent of the US population now is 2.1 million people; in 1933 it was 1.25 million.

The foregoing observations on the role of population have been strictly arithmetical ones, with no attention to the possible cause-and-effect relations between population and the other factors contributing to pressures on resources and environment, and no consideration of possible differences in the response of the environment and the society to successive increments of impact. It is in these possibilities, however, that the greatest potential for harm in further population growth resides. Consider some of the ways in which changes in demographic variables can cause changes in consumption per capita and in pollution per unit of consumption. The present spatial pattern of population growth —suburbanization—leads to increased use of the automobile (more vehicle miles per person). This effect, together with that of population density itself, leads in turn to increased traffic congestion, hence more gallons of gasoline and harmful emissions per vehicle mile, and longer periods that the drivers are exposed to elevated concentrations of pollutants. The demand of each new increment of population for food is met by means of disproportionate increases in the use of fertilizer and pesticides on existing land; a 1 percent increase in output now requires increases in inputs much greater than 1 percent—an example of diminishing returns. Growing demand for materials and fuels—the combined result of population growth and rising affluence—accelerates the application of more energy-intensive and environmentally disruptive techniques needed to exploit lower grade ores. In all these cases, population growth is generating pressures, directly and indirectly, that grow faster than the population itself.

A further 30 percent increase in the population of the United States, then, is likely to cause an increase in pressure on resources and environment that considerably exceeds 30 percent. The threat is compounded by the fact that the response of any system, environmental or social, may change dramatically with rather small changes in pressure as its capacity is approached. That is, the next 5 percent may cause a very different response than the previous 5 percent. Such thresholds are not uncommon in everyday experience —the difference between a freeway carrying a capacity load at sixty miles per hour and a massive traffic jam is a few extra cars; and they are not uncommon in nature—fish that tolerate a ten degree rise in temperature without difficulty may turn belly up when the temperature goes up five degrees more. Neither the thresholds of . . . environmental systems . . . nor those of our social systems have yet been identified, but symptoms of stress in both areas are abundant enough that it seems imprudent, to say the least, to regard *any* further increase in population-related pressures with complacency.

FALLOUT FROM ZPG [9]

The art of societal guidance is still in a rather primitive stage. Not only do we rarely get where we set out to go, but when we do get there we often find that we've made a serious mistake—that what we've achieved is not at all what we aspired to. Among the values we once cherished, and urged on other countries, are rapid economic growth, strong technology, and material wealth. All are now being questioned. While this is not yet the case for Zero Population Growth (ZPG), it may be soon, at least for the United States.

Figures released in March 1973 show that the number of births in the USA in 1972 was the smallest in twenty-seven years. The decline continues to be sharp: 10 per cent in one year, since 1971, according to the New York *Times*. Moreover, the *Times* indicates that the fertility rate (the average number of children a woman has over her lifetime) fell, for the first time since God knows when, below the [2.11] mark to an average of 2.03 for 1972. This drop is highly significant, as it brought the American birthrate below the "replacement level" of [2.11] children. Theoretically, that puts us not just in ZPG, but into DPG (Declining Population Growth). [For another view, see "The Birthrate Falls" in Section I, above.—Ed.] No one can predict with certainty whether these low rates will persist, spiral back up, or drop even further. But the nature of the forces that seem to push them down—the increasing number of women who work, the rise in the divorce rate, the changing values (we

[9] Article "Zero Population Growth: Do We Really Want It?" by Amitai Etzioni, professor of sociology, Columbia University; director, Center for Policy Research; author of *The Active Society,* and recently, *The Genetic Fix. Evaluation.* v 1, no 2:84-5. Summer '73. Reprinted by permission.

even question Motherhood!)—may well continue and extend their sway.

So it is high time to ask, now that we're getting a taste of what ZPG entails, do we really want more of it? If it's here to stay, we ought to take advantage of this "introductory period" to reexamine ZPG's blessings from a closer range.

We have been conditioned by years of intensive campaigns to view population growth as a source of many evils, including crowding, tough competition over ever scarcer resources, war, low standards of living, and so on. But as with most propagandistic campaigns, the fight for smaller families has looked away from the less attractive facets of the goal. These facets can no longer be avoided.

A stabilized or declining population has the following attributes:

1. It is an ever older population, with more senior citizens, fewer children, and fewer young adults. While there were about 4 million first graders starting school in September 1968, by 1978, says the *Times,* there will be only 3.2 million. (In colleges, according to the *Chronicle of Higher Education,* for reasons such as the ending of the draft and the rising costs of tuition, college enrollments are already decelerating from a 12 per cent peak in 1965 to only 2 per cent in Fall 1972.)

On the other hand, nursing homes for the aged, hospitals, and other facilities catering to senior citizens will be in increasing demand and probably crowded. Thirty percent of our population is now under fifteen, and those over sixty-five constitute only 10 percent, but Leslie and Charles Westhoff calculate that in a population of zero growth-rate, by the year 2000 the proportion of people over sixty-five would be equal to that of those under fifteen.

An aging population also has spiraling health costs. Not only are older people more illness-prone, they are also less able to pay for their medical costs. Thus, fewer and fewer productive Americans will be required to foot the bill for more and more retiring, aging, often not-well Americans.

2. The recent trend to delay marriage, delay having children, and space children more widely may offer the mother greater independence and career opportunities, but will sharply increase the number of children born with genetic deformities such as mongolism, for as I point out in *The Genetic Fix* . . . (Macmillan, 1973), the probability that a deformed child will be born increases as the mother gets older.

3. The relationship between population growth and economic growth is complex, but basically, although a decline in population might result in an increase in individual standard of living, it will also tend to bring about less demand and a slacking economy. The loss of young workers (due to the aging population) will be balanced by an increase of women who are no longer tied to maternal chores. But once the new employment of women levels off, when as many of them as wish are at work, "the economy," *Fortune* says, can grow "only as fast as the average output per worker. This means that if productivity is still rising at 3 per cent or so a year with the population stabilized, the economy's potential rate of growth would be 3 per cent a year rather than the present rate of more than 4 per cent."

4. A stabilized rate of growth also has political implications. An expanding economy provides a greater opportunity for peaceful settlement of conflicts; more can be given to satisfy new demands, without anyone sacrificing anything. In contrast, a stable or shrinking economy intensifies tensions and conflicts because one cannot give a share to any newly active group or newly recognized need without cutting someone else's share.

5. The fact that birth control is more accepted and practiced in some ethnic groups, racial groups, or social classes than in others, suggests that, as is the case now, the lower classes and the disadvantaged groups will continue to grow more rapidly than the rest of the society. This will continue

to strain the facilities available to lower class and minority people and create a demand for population curbs on the more rapidly growing groups. This would in effect constitute some sort of selective population control, which, Robert Buckhout points out, is the view of ZPG already held by blacks and Chicanos in the USA.

All this is not to say that ZPG is without virtue. But many seem to have accepted the simple formula that if a growing number of people are closing in on a shrinking amount of resources, the problem could be reduced by reducing the number of people. The recent energy crisis only seems to highlight the need for such an approach.

Unfortunately it is not that simple. Demand on resources is determined by how much each person spends, in addition to how many spenders there are. Thus, for example, if we have a 2 per cent population decline a year (a rather sizeable decline), but the remaining people increase their consumption by 3 per cent (a common phenomenon), the demand on resources will continue to rise along with the blessed ZPG, let alone with the DPG. As someone put it, the problem is not people, but rich people.

Disregarded, too, is the fact that if there will be fewer young producers and more older consumers—an almost inevitable result of a stabilized population and prolonged life expectancy—there will be less to go around. And, with the increased consumer power of the individual, coupled with the lower gross national product, the scarcity will continue.

I personally believe that the promise of ZPG for affluent industrial societies like ours has been widely exaggerated and that more rapid, more effective, and less costly solutions to our problems could be achieved by technological progress. For instance, the new ways of using nuclear energy could provide us with all the energy we can use at reasonable economic and social costs. In any event, our primary concern should be not material welfare, but the more elusive and complex problem of spiritual, social, and personal development. If we don't shift our emphasis from materialism to genuine growth, ZPG or not, none of our main problems will be resolved.

I am not quite ready to argue that a slowly rising population is, all around, better for America than ZPG. But neither should we semihysterically push for ZPG, only to discover—after millions of lives are affected and billions spent—that SRPG (Slowly Rising Population Growth) is more desirable, at which point we will then probably oversteer in the opposite direction, demanding larger families in a hurry. We need to establish national commissions that will carefully review societal goals and programs before we actively endorse them. These commissions should be bipartisan and appointed by the Congress, not the White House. They should be composed of experts, humanists, and community leaders. Their work should be backed up by a research staff. And they should hold public hearings as a way to stir up and feed a national debate. For unless we find a more responsible way of evaluating and implementing national goals, most of our efforts will turn against us.

IS THERE A POPULATION POLICY? [10]

The United States is taking the first tentative steps toward development of a national population policy. With the upsurge of concern over the condition of the physical environment plus the great difficulties in solving US social problems there has been rising feeling that a third hundred-million people could be accommodated in this nation only under environmental and social conditions that many people are now unwilling to accept.

Even with the lowered fertility rate of the last decade and the reduction in the number of children young married women say they want, the population is expected to grow through the next hundred years because of the great num-

[10] Summary from pamphlet entitled *More?* League of Women Voters of the United States. 1730 M St. N.W. Washington, D.C. 20036. '72. p 33-5. © 1972 by The League of Women Voters of the United States. Reprinted by permission.

ber of young people entering the family-forming years. Only a great change in US attitudes toward marriage and children could prevent this increase.

Contrary to the prevailing mythology, it is not the exceptionally large family and not the poor families who have most of the children, but it is the great number of families who have a third child, or a fourth, that keep the fertility rate higher than is needed for replacement. [See "The Birthrate Falls," in Section I, above.—Ed.] Supporters of family planning believe that population growth would be substantially reduced if the means to prevent the birth of all unwanted children were fully available. Some of them add that if *voluntary* birth control is to work, it will be essential to provide other and equally rewarding alternatives for women to keep them from wanting the additional child or two.

Motivation and inducement toward smaller families are being discussed, but no serious US governmental consideration has been given to compulsory restriction of family size. Governmental programs have been launched to give poor people and rural people the same opportunity to decide on the number and spacing of children as people with financial resources and available health services enjoy. Freedom of choice programs are criticized for what they do and for what they don't do. In any case, many people are still not reached.

Population distribution is receiving attention, with balanced growth becoming an "in" phrase. The single most startling fact is most Americans now live in suburbs. Only a small proportion are rural people and very few of these are farm people. The big metropolitan agglomerations—BoWash [Boston to Washington, D.C.] ChiPitts [Chicago to Pittsburgh], and SanSan [San Francisco to San Diego]—are expected to continue to attract people, chiefly migrants from other urban areas, but to grow, as all urban areas do, mostly by natural increase.

New towns and the enlargement of existing growth centers (dispersed, middle-sized cities) are seen as the most feasible means of attracting people away from the huge . . . [metropolitan areas]. Job opportunities are the key, for most movement is toward job attractions within metro areas. So far neither new towns nor growth centers have made any appreciable change in the trend toward population concentration in metropolitan areas.

No one knows whether US population growth will exceed the nation's scientific, technological, and industrial ability to provide adequately for all the people. We do know that growth cannot go on forever. Historically, the standard of living has gone up, but the requirements of more and more people, with the exponential growth of side effects from domestic and industrial wastes, could bring down our relative affluence. Serious consideration is being given to the benefits of slower economic growth and a more stable population. There is significant support, in fact, for the view that altered economic growth-patterns offer the fastest route to short-range management of our environmental problems. Although not imminent, the time for population stabilization will surely come.

There is growing acceptance of the concept that man is part of an ecosystem whose delicate balance can be upset by uncontrolled growth of people and things. People are looking askance at the consequences of suburban sprawl and center-city decay. They ask whether the public's discomfort and lost opportunities have been figured into the bill. People are wondering whether these social costs could be avoided and the needs of the population met with careful environmental planning. They ask whether a pervasive and systematic assessment should be made of technology to identify social costs and benefits of its new and existing applications. People are looking at more than technical and economic feasibility or cost/benefit ratios in evaluating programs and policies. They ask whether quality will be served, whether use of virgin resources can be reduced and a "spaceship earth" economy encouraged.

The people of the United States are only at the beginning of their consideration of a national growth policy. Changes in behavioral patterns and in social mores take a long time. As we see the importance to the welfare of society, a new social ethic, widely understood and accepted, may develop, an ethic including smaller families and satisfaction from fewer material possessions.

Now is the time for a reasoned and informed public discourse on the issues painted here in broad strokes. Now is the time to move toward consensus on governmental policy, toward programs that implement that policy coherently.

III. QUESTIONS OF MORALS

EDITOR'S INTRODUCTION

This section deals mainly with the moral problems involved in reducing the number of births. It begins with an extract from an article in *Family Planning Perspectives,* published by Planned Parenthood. Larry Bumpass and Charles F. Westoff examined how many births were unwanted, concluding that prevention of these births would have substantially cut the US birthrate. There follows an opinion by Representative John N. Erlenborn of Illinois objecting to contraceptive services to sexually active teenagers and to abortion on request. Then comes the Washington *Post* story on the decision of the United States Supreme Court in 1973 that legalized abortion. Arlie Schardt, writing in *Civil Liberties,* the organ of the American Civil Liberties Union, reports on the strength of the influences being brought to bear on Congress on behalf of a constitutional amendment barring abortion.

Excerpts from a pamphlet issued by the Division of Family Life, United States Catholic Conference, argue for life-enhancing measures and particularly against any dictation on the size of one's family except by one's conscience; also condemned is any resort to abortion.

Next comes the portion of the Population Commission's report that advocates contraceptive services for sexually active teenagers. This is endorsed by a statement from Planned Parenthood. In the following article from *Parents' Magazine,* Eric W. Johnson sets forth a proposed sex education program for use in schools. An argument is then presented by the Council for Basic Education opposing sex education in schools.

UNWANTED BIRTHS [1]

To formulate appropriate population policy, it is necessary first to evaluate the relative importance of the different components of population growth. If most US population growth were due to immigration, for example, one set of remedial policies might ensue. If our growth were due mainly to wanted babies born to couples who practice modern contraception, then another set of policies might be indicated. If our growth were substantially accounted for by unwanted pregnancies among couples who practice either no contraception or inadequate contraception, then a third and quite different set of policies might be suggested.

The responses of a representative national sample of some 5,600 women interviewed for the 1965 National Fertility Study has made possible an informed estimate of the extent of unwanted fertility in the period from 1960 to 1965. These are births described by respondents as "unwanted" at the time of their conception by either the father, the mother or both. They provide the basis for estimating the number of births that might not have occurred if the couples had access to perfect contraception.

Analysis of these data has led to a number of provocative conclusions. Most important, it is evident that a large proportion of recent births to married couples was unwanted; and that if only wanted babies had been born, the US birthrate and thus, the rate of population growth would have been substantially reduced. . . .

About one fifth of all births and more than one third of Negro births which occurred from 1960 to 1965 were unwanted. This is a "medium" estimate; the percent reported

[1] From "Unwanted Births and U.S. Population Growth," by Larry Bumpass, assistant professor of sociology, University of Wisconsin, and Charles F. Westoff, professor of sociology, Princeton University. *Family Planning Perspectives.* 2:9-11. O. '70. Reprinted with permission from *Family Planning Perspectives*, v 2, no 4, April 1970.

unwanted by at least one spouse was slightly higher—22 percent of all births and 41 percent of Negro births.

As would be expected, the percent unwanted increases rapidly by birth order: 5 percent of first births, 30 percent of fourth births and 50 percent of sixth or higher order births were reported as unwanted. For Negroes the corresponding figures are 12 percent, 44 percent and 66 percent. The high rates for Negroes underscore the magnitude of the unwanted burden of dependents that is borne by this population, although the problems of unwanted fertility are very substantial among whites as well.

As would be expected the incidence of unwanted births varies inversely with education and income. In general the proportion of births unwanted is approximately twice as high among wives with less than a high school education as among women who have attended college.

In terms of the Social Security Administration's definition of poverty, near-poverty and nonpoverty, the incidence of unwanted births is very much higher among the poor and near-poor. Fifteen percent of births to nonpoor families were declared unwanted, compared to 23 percent among the near-poor and 37 percent among the poor. (Or 32 percent for poor and near-poor taken together.) Three fifths of all sixth or higher order births among the poor were unwanted.

Since family size is one component of the SSA [Social Security Administration] definition of poverty, many couples would not have been classified as poor were it not for their fertility experience. The results, therefore, indicate the coincidence of poverty and unwanted fertility rather than any "propensity" of the poor to have unwanted births.

For the six years from 1960 to 1965, these proportions yield a medium estimate of 4.7 million unwanted births in all socioeconomic groups. Approximately two million of these unwanted births occurred among the poor and near-poor.

It seems clear that the prevention of unwanted fertility

would have had a substantial impact on the US birthrate, and consequently on the population growth rate over the six-year period, 1960-1965.

The potential impact of the elimination of unwanted fertility on our future growth rate will depend on the number of children that women now entering the child-bearing age group will ultimately want to have. For those women who were near the end of childbearing in 1965 (ages thirty-five to forty-four), the elimination of unwanted births would have reduced their fertility from 3.0 to 2.5 births per woman. Since to achieve a zero rate of population growth would require an average fertility of 2.25 children per woman, the elimination of unwanted births would not have been sufficient to establish exact replacement, but it would have made considerable progress toward this objective.

These estimates are likely to be too low as a result of the reporting of originally unwanted births as wanted. It must be difficult for a woman retrospectively to report a birth as unwanted since such a report reflects on her ability to control her fertility, and perhaps also on the status of the child who is now a member of the family. Another source of underestimation is that this analysis is based on a sample of married women living with their husbands in 1965. Births to women not living with their husbands and most illegitimate births are not represented. The estimates made in this article assume that the incidence and birth-order distribution of all unwanted births is the same as those reported by wives now living with their husbands. This undoubtedly is a bias in the direction of underestimating the extent of unwanted fertility.

Timing Failures

It is difficult to assess the long-term effects of timing failures (that is, births occurring before they are wanted) on population growth. It has been suggested that the longer a "wanted" birth is delayed, the less likely a woman is to have that birth or a subsequent birth. This is because the delay provides the woman time to assume roles which are not compatible with early childcare responsibility, and also increases the likelihood that she or her husband will become subfecund. . . .

More than two fifths of "wanted" births which occurred from 1960 to 1965 were reported by the parents as "timing failures."

Policy Implications

We estimate that if women near the end of childbearing in 1965 could have avoided unwanted births they would have come much closer than they did to attaining cohort replacement. It is of course possible that women now entering the childbearing ages will choose to have more children than were wanted by women of the same age in the high fertility period of the early 1950s. It is not, however, likely. The oral contraceptives have continued to be rapidly diffused since 1965, and this diffusion may well reduce the numbers of "desired" as well as unwanted children. Women may prefer smaller families as they are increasingly enabled to enter into nonfamilial roles (particularly employment) than they would otherwise have chosen. Indeed, there are already indications that the completed fertility of the most recent cohorts of women will be lower than that of those which preceded it. It seems likely that today's young women would have a completed fertility, given the elimination of all unwanted births, below that inferred for women who were thirty-five to forty-four in 1965 under the same assumption.

The elimination of unwanted fertility is an important goal in human terms as well as in terms of its potential impact on future US population growth. Social policies to accomplish this would include:

Significant expansion of research to develop more effective means of fertility control

Development of more efficient systems of distribution of contraceptive methods among all Americans, including those low-income couples who have not had access thus far to effective family planning

Legalization of abortion on request as a backup measure in cases of failed contraception, and appropriate policies to make abortion available to all who need it, regardless of socioeconomic status

If the fertility patterns of the last decade continue, these three measures by themselves might reduce US population growth considerably. They would not require any change in the number of children couples appear to want now, and thus, would not require governmental policies designed to change family-size norms. No alternative population control measures which have been proposed appear to hold out as much promise of a reduction in US population growth. It seems apparent therefore, that a major program along these lines would be a significant element in any national program to reduce population growth.

A DISSENTING OPINION [2]

I am compelled at the outset . . . to offer an observation: I do not believe the Report [of the Commission or Population Growth and the American Future] is proposing that contraceptive devices be sold through vending machines in school corridors, and I hope it will not be so construed.

As to contraception, the law, and minors, I wish the Commission had applied an age qualification to the term minor. Even so, I cannot join in the Commission's recommendation that all legal restrictions on access to contraceptive information and services should be eliminated to permit minors, youngsters under the age at which they are legally responsible for themselves, unlimited access to contraceptives and abortions.

[2] Dissenting opinion by Representative John N. Erlenborn (Republican, Illinois). In *Population and the American Future: The Report of the Commission on Population Growth and the American Future.* Supt. of Docs. Washington, D.C. 20402. '72. p 156-7.

As I have stated elsewhere, the goal of increasing the quality of life should not be paramount to the sanctity of life. The exercise of any right in excess can lead to license.

Throughout this Report, the emphasis on the rights of the individual is used to justify increased individual freedom and responsibility. Yet, the facts cited in the Report, particularly when dealing with questions of minors, show that minors are often inexperienced and ill-equipped to deal with the questions that the new freedom gives them.

I would have preferred that the Commission qualify its recommendation to give greater weight to circumstances and the need for parental guidance. I can fully support the recommendations that the consequences of illegitimacy and teenage pregnancy be reduced so that the mother will have a chance of enjoying a satisfying life. The tensions associated with what is, perhaps, an unwanted pregnancy should be reduced. At the same time, however, we should not detach ourselves, as the Commission does, from the related moral and social questions.

By eliminating any need or concern for parental guidance, the Commission essentially takes the view that the child knows better than the parent what his rights and responsibilities are. This, in my view, goes too far in placing emphasis on individual right, and tends to ignore responsibility for one's own actions.

A particular fear haunts me with regard to the lack of a recommendation that teenagers be exempted from laws permitting voluntary sterilization beyond the assumption that usual and accepted medical judgment will be exercised.

I do not know of any age a human being passes through that is more impressionable, more susceptible to suggestion, than the teen years. To couple this impressionability with access to sterilization without parental guidance can mean that many youngsters, in their zeal to be patriotic, to do something for mankind, will know more than a few moments of torment and regret.

It is no answer, to my mind, to these young people and

others merely to suggest that sperm banks can alleviate concern about a change of mind. Technology in this area has not advanced to the stage that permits this guarantee. And, finally, the moral questions posed by artificial insemination remain unresolved.

Abortion

I cannot accept the recommendation that present state abortion laws be liberalized to allow abortions to be performed on request.

My basic premise is that we must include within our concern for the quality and enhancement of life a respect for life itself—indeed, it should be paramount. Otherwise, the concern for the enhancement or enrichment of life is entirely materialistic. Thus, I believe the Report should have resolved the moral and ethical issues it raised. The Report could have served a useful purpose at this point by a more wide-ranging discussion of these issues. Instead, it does nothing to clarify the fundamental bases on which people now quite rightly object to liberalized abortion.

A discussion of the moral and ethical issues, I realize, is not an easy task. How, for instance, do we distinguish between abortion and infanticide? The goal of relieving the mother of the burdens of child-rearing is the same; thus, some distinction between the means must lead to a recommendation of the one and not the other.

At what point in the development of the fetus do we consider it to be human life worthy of the protection of society? And what event signals the change of the fetus from the state of nonhuman to human? My own view is that the fetus is a new, separate human being from the moment of conception.

It would be helpful for those reading this Report to be able to review the reasoning leading to the judgment that liberal abortion is morally defensible. In my own view, it is difficult, if not impossible, to reach that moral judgment, and yet stop short of justifying infanticide, euthanasia, or the killing of the severely mentally or physically handicapped.

I believe that the failure of the text to resolve these questions of moral judgment places the recommendation outside a moral context.

Viewed within a moral or ethical context, I do not believe that this society can accept the destruction of human life for the comfort or convenience of individuals within the society.

Complexity of Situations

Furthermore, the recommendations do not reflect the complexity of potential situations in which abortion may be called for. It does not distinguish, for example, between the rights of married and unmarried women to request abortion. What may be appropriate for an unmarried woman to decide between herself and her doctor may be completely inappropriate for a married woman, who thus ignores the rights of her husband. Moreover, there are numerous distinctions of a medical nature which could be made to limit the scope of the recommendation.

In this section, the Commission notes the difficulty of assessing the demographic impact of liberalized abortion. Its impact would be small, no doubt less than that of immigration. And yet, abortion on request takes precedence as a recommendation over one concerning the limiting of immigration. Since this is a "Population" Commission and not a "Birth Control" Commission, what compelling consideration leads the Commission to make this very controversial recommendation when it has little or no population or demographic consequence?

In summary, for all of the reasons noted, I find it impossible to join with the Commission in these recommendations.

ABORTION RULED LEGAL [3]

Striking down the antiabortion laws of most of the states, the Supreme Court ruled [in January 1973] that a woman has an absolute right during her first three months of pregnancy to decide whether to bear her child.

Between the third and seventh months of pregnancy, the court held, states have power to regulate the medical aspects of abortion. After the twenty-sixth or twenty-seventh week of pregnancy, the states may forbid all abortions except those essential to save the mother's life or health.

More than forty states . . . have laws similar to those of Texas or Georgia, whose laws were nullified [by the Court]. If they want to reassert the power to control abortions at all, these states will have to pass new laws.

Justice Harry A. Blackmun, writing for a 7 to 2 majority, said the mother's "qualified right," admittedly never before recognized by the high court, was grounded in the Fourteenth Amendment's safeguards of personal liberty, including the right to privacy.

Dissenting Justices Byron R. White and William H. Rehnquist accused the majority of using "raw judicial power" to exalt "the convenience, whim or caprice of the putative mother" over valued interests of the states and society.

Although the court emphasized that it was not declaring any right to "abortion on demand," the only major limitation on the mother's freedom was the requirement that a licensed physician agree to perform the operation.

Leaders of the effort to ease restrictions on abortion were jubilant. Some women's liberation advocates, while reluctant to concede any governmental power on the question, also voiced approval.

Spokesmen for the Catholic Church denounced the decision in bitter terms.

[3] From "Supreme Court Allows Early-Stage Abortions," by John P. Mackenzie, staff correspondent. Washington *Post.* p 1. Ja. 23, '73. © 1973 by The Washington Post. Reprinted by permission.

John Cardinal Krol of Philadelphia, president of the National Conference of Catholic Bishops, called the ruling "an unspeakable tragedy for this nation" and "a monstrous injustice." He added: "The ruling drastically diminishes the constitutional guarantee of the right to life and in doing so sets in motion developments which are terrifying to contemplate."

The court specifically rejected claims of a "right to life" of the unborn.

SAVING ABORTION [4]

When the Supreme Court legalized abortion . . . [in] January [1973] with a pair of sweeping, 7-2 rulings, many people relaxed. They believed the issue was settled, and that henceforth the state could not interfere with a woman's right to decide with her doctor whether or not to terminate her pregnancy.

Such people could not have been more mistaken. Far from settling the issue, that decision—undoubtedly the most controversial and far-reaching since *Brown* v. *Board of Education* outlawed school segregation in 1954—set off a wave of reaction among certain groups:

At least 188 antiabortion bills have been introduced in 41 states.

Several states have enacted, or are retaining, antiabortion laws which are clearly unconstitutional, but are being invoked nonetheless.

Approximately 10 per cent of the United States House of Representatives (some 41 of the House's 435 members) are sponsoring some form of antiabortion legislation.

Although opponents know they can only overthrow the Supreme Court decisions by passing a constitutional amendment, the availability of abortion has already

[4] From "New Threats: Saving Abortion," by Arlie Schardt. *Civil Liberties.* No. 298:1-2. S. '73. Reprinted by permission.

been reduced via amendments to other bills passed by Congress.

Three distinct types of constitutional amendments have been put before the Congress, including one sponsored by seven senators.

A discharge petition (the same device used . . . [in 1972] in the school busing controversy) has been introduced in the House, seeking to dislodge one of the proposed constitutional amendments from committee and put it directly on the House floor.

Cost of Silence

The proponents of these laws have been flooding their legislators with mail. Some members of Congress receive more mail opposing abortion than on any other subject. Because those who favor abortion mistakenly believe the Court has settled the issue, they have not been writing at all. Their silence, if continued, will prove costly.

Among the many ironies attending the issue, two stand out. First, continued inaction by proabortion citizens could result in the Court's decision being overthrown through passage of a constitutional amendment by a panicky Congress, even though polls show most Americans favor a woman's right to choose abortion. The last nationwide poll, taken by Gallup in June 1972, found 64 per cent agreeing that abortion is a decision solely for a woman and her doctor. A Gallup poll in January 1972, also found 54 per cent of Catholics of the same opinion.

Second, enactment of a constitutional amendment to prohibit abortion will not eliminate abortion, or even reduce it. It will only turn back the nation to the pre-1973 days when millions of women underwent illegal abortions, often under unsafe conditions. Many suffered serious injury or death as a result. Prohibition of abortion has been no more effective than prohibition of alcohol was in the 1930s.

History of Laws

Compounding these ironies is the fact that any new abortion law would be a complete contradiction of the reason why abortion laws were first introduced into English and American common law at all. That reason was to protect women from the dangers posed by medical conditions of those times. Such protection is no longer needed because today abortion is safer than childbirth. This has been true, in fact, since approximately 1930. Abortion laws have thus been counterproductive for some forty years, because they no longer protect the patient's life, as intended. Indeed, they actually deny the protection they were meant to provide. Studies made after New York State liberalized its abortion laws in 1970, for example, indicate that eight times more women per 100,000 died in childbirth than as the result of legal abortions performed within the first twenty-four weeks of pregnancy.

The common-law liberty of women to have abortions existed in England from 1327 to 1803, and in America from 1607 to 1830. Abortion was legal when the United States Constitution was written in 1789, thus making it a woman's right under the Ninth Amendment, which says the enumeration of certain rights in the Constitution shall not be construed to deny others.

When legislatures began passing abortion laws in the 1800s, the motive was neither religion nor morality. The laws did not seek to discourage sexual promiscuity, since they applied to married as well as unmarried women, and to victims of rape. Nor did they seek to protect the fetus. [Their object was to protect women from the dangerous medical techniques of the time.—Ed.]

Rights of Fetus

This last concept [of protecting the fetus]—the effort to establish the fetus as a person with full legal rights—has become the rallying cry of the "right to life" groups spearheading the antiabortion campaign's drive for a constitutional amendment.

Their motive has been questioned by others, who charge that the antiabortion campaign is really an attempt to impose one religion's beliefs on the lives of all. They point out that vigorous lobbying is being conducted by such official bodies as the U.S. Catholic Conference and the National Conference of Catholic Bishops, and that the membership of the primary citizen lobby, the National Right to Life Committee (NRLC), is overwhelmingly Catholic. The NRLC denies any religious motivation, stating its only concern is the sanctity of all life.

The January [1973] Supreme Court rulings, which antiabortionists seek to overturn, were an expansion of the privacy doctrine through which the Court had earlier determined that persons may not be hampered by the state in their access to contraceptives. There, Justice Brennan wrote for the Court in *Eisenstadt* v. *Baird* that "If the right of privacy means anything, it is the right of the individual, married or single, to be free from unwarranted governmental intrusion into matters so fundamentally affecting a person as the decision whether to bear or beget a child."

A CATHOLIC VIEWPOINT [5]

Population growth and distribution and the allocation of resources to meet the needs of people are matters which demand serious thought and study. Much visibility was given to population questions during the 1960s, and public attention must be expected to increase during the decade of the 1970s. The United Nations has designated 1974 as UN Population Year. This will provide maximum visibility for every aspect of the population question.

[5] From pamphlet *Respect Life!* United States Catholic Conference. Division of Family Life. 1312 Massachusetts Ave. N.W. Washington, D.C. 20005. '73. p 38-43. Reprinted with permission. Respect Life is a program of the National Conference of Catholic Bishops, conducted under the auspices of the NCCB Committee for Population and Pro-Life Activities.

Population Dynamics

Two central factors determine the rate of population growth in a given nation—the birthrate and the death rate. When life expectancy is short and a large proportion of children die before adolescence, high birthrates are almost necessary and the rate of population growth is low and fairly constant. When life expectancy is increased and improved medical services lower the death rate, the continued high birthrate results in high and sometimes explosive population growth. The effect of population growth is then felt on food resources, on health and education facilities, on economic and employment structures. In developing nations, rapid population growth often renders difficult or complicates efforts to industrialize, to develop natural resources and establish effective social structures.

Another important factor influencing population growth is migration. When large numbers of young people leave a country, population growth may be out of line with projections based only on birthrates and death rates. And when large numbers of immigrants enter a nation each year, they account for an increase over and above that attributable to fertility. At present, immigration accounts for more than 20 percent of America's annual population increase.

Decisions regarding population growth are both societal and personal. On the societal level, governments might adopt laws or policies calculated to influence the decisions of couples regarding the size of the family or the frequency of births. Examples of such governmental activity would include laws governing the age at marriage, tax laws regulating the number of children for whom an income tax deduction will be allowed, laws determining maximum number of children eligible in each family for education or health care benefits. In a more subtle fashion, government policy regarding the size of apartment houses or mortgage guarantees for single-family dwellings will have some influence on the size of families. Of course, government encouragement of abortion and sterilization as means of fertility control, or the adding of some antifertility agent to the water supply would have more direct and coercive effects on fertility patterns.

On the other hand, the personal values of parents will result in decisions concerning family size, and the cumulative effect on these value-oriented decisions will determine the national birthrate. In agricultural societies, each child becomes a working member of the family quite early in life, and provides some assurance that the older members of the society will be cared for. In an industrial and highly mobile society, educating children to enable them to make their own way is costly for parents. Moreover, as the society becomes more technological, employment patterns change, and parents face great uncertainty as to the future of each child they bring into the world.

Still, most parents are somewhat optimistic about the future. Their sacrifices in childbearing and child rearing are rewarded by their children's love and accomplishments, and the satisfaction of family life. Parents do not generally look on their children as statistics, pollutants, or threats to the storehouse of natural resources. They look at them quite simply as children, as bearers of promise, and as a link with the future. Consequently, personal decisions regarding family size are generally based on the health of the parents, the family's income, judgments as to necessities and luxuries and the ability of parents to provide them. Fertility decisions reflect the individual couple's own sense of priorities, and their willingness to sacrifice personal desires for the sake of parenthood.

Until the modern era, the birthrate fairly well reflected the choices—and capabilities—of married couples. And these choices were generally considered to be private and personal. But in recent years considerable attention has been given to the finite character of the world and its natural resources, to the increased damage to the natural environment, and to the new perception of the status of woman and her right to equal opportunity. The result has been a strong and highly visible campaign for zero population growth, coupled with demands that the government take a more direct role in bringing about lower fertility rates.

The following points give a brief overview of the population question in the United States during the last decade:

1. The birthrate and the new growth rate of the American population have been generally decreasing since the late 1950s. . . . United States Census Bureau estimates [for 1973] indicate that the . . . [fertility] rate is now at 1.97 children per family, well below the rate of 2.11 which equals . . . population stabilization. [But see "Fertility Up Slightly in 1973," in Section I, above.—Ed.]

2. The birth expectations of American women have shown a similar decrease, particularly since 1967, and especially among younger women eighteen to twenty-four years of age.

3. The fertility of Catholic women has declined to the same degree as the overall population, and some recent studies of wanted fertility indicate a more significant decline among Catholic women. This finding is supported by Census Bureau reports of fertility variations by ethnic origin.

4. Fertility rates are appreciably higher among women of Mexican and Puerto Rican origin than the overall population, with those of Mexican origin being the highest.

5. During the 1960s, the dominant concern of American governmental programs was to provide family planning services to the poor so that poor families could achieve their fertility goals. It was assumed that unwanted fertility among the poor and minority groups was appreciably higher because of lack of family planning assistance.

6. During the 1970s, concern has shifted to establishment of population policy, and an educational effort directed to all segments of the population. Unwanted fertility is still an important target, but greater emphasis is being

placed on small family size as a primary social goal. Greater incentives are being offered to limit family size to two children. These incentives are tied to the achievement of other social goals such as ecological improvement, more education, increased leisure, adaptation to a projected decrease of employment opportunity, etc. In effect, the basis of judgment as to wanted childbearing has shifted from fulfilling personal family goals to the fulfillment of highly publicized social goals.

Population—The World Problem

In the United States, and in most industrialized countries, rapid population growth is not a serious problem. In fact, in most nations of the world the rate of population increase has been declining during the 1960s. But many developing nations, particularly India, the Philippines, and many countries in Africa and South America, have relatively high annual rates of population increase. In such countries, the rates of population increase tend to outdistance the nation's ability to develop industrially, to achieve widespread education and to deliver health care to all. There is little question that a limitation of population growth in some developing nations would be a distinct advantage, and in some cases it is a dire necessity.

The higher the rate of population growth, the more rapidly a population doubles. The "doubling" process has an effect on other aspects of a nation's development. The basic statistics of population growth—i.e., birthrates, death rates, immigration and annual rate of population increase— tell only part of the story. The statistics must be correlated with other factors that give us some idea of how a nation can cope with population growth. These other factors include:

Food Production and Distribution. It was commonly assumed that rapid population growth would exhaust food supplies and cause famine, resulting in the death of millions of people from starvation and/or malnutrition. In recent years, the "Green Revolution"—the development of new seeds and fertilizers—has given us the capability of producing massive amounts of food, even in nations with a poor agricultural history. Although the present forecasts are more positive, the distribution of food remains a problem. Drought, war or natural catastrophes such as earthquakes or storms can temporarily cancel or forestall agricultural gains.

Employment. Development for every nation involves some degree of industrialization, and industrialization can mean jobs. However, the developing nations usually emphasize agriculture and have only a small (but growing) industrial component. Unemployment runs high, especially as more people congregate in the cities looking for work. A lower birthrate would not lower the unemployment rate, but it might allow a better distribution of the gross national product, and a better deployment of the work force. Yet, the developed nations with low population growth end up importing labor from neighboring countries because of lack of people or gaps in the age-structure of their own populations.

Housing. In almost all nations, housing is insufficient and costly. This is partially due to urbanization, that is, the localizing of business and industry close to the big cities. It is also due to the fact that low- and middle-income housing is not financially rewarding for investors, with the result that the dwellings which are built are for the wealthier segments of the population. The provision of adequate housing remains a problem in almost every nation in the world.

Health Care. Most developing nations simply do not have a modern health-care delivery system. There is a shortage of doctors, nurses and health-care personnel, as well as hospitals and other facilities. This generally results in greater disease and higher death rates among the poorest people, who also tend to have larger families so that some children will survive.

Education. Although educational facilities have increased during this century in every part of the world, illiteracy is still widespread in the poor or developing nations. Thus personal development is stifled, and large groups of people are unable to improve their living conditions simply because they do not know how to do so. Yet, as educational attainment rises, family size tends to decrease.

Population and the Environment. Population increase is often blamed as a major cause of environmental pollution. The argument is that the excessive number of people on earth is exhausting natural resources, that people are polluting the rivers and streams, filling the atmosphere with smoke and fumes, destroying the landscape with highways and parking lots. But as the National Academy of Sciences notes: "There is little doubt that, at least in the developed countries, sheer numbers are not nearly as important in causing pollution as are the high levels of consumption and the by-products of a highly developed and diversified technology."

These brief and very general comments point to aspects of man's life in society that may be aggravated by rapid population increase and continued high rates of population growth. In each case, population is not the causal factor, nor would the lowering of population necessarily solve the particular social problem. In fact, in some cases, moderate population growth is necessary to solve a nation's problems. In general, however, it can be said that specific efforts to increase food production and distribution, efforts to create and distribute jobs, massive efforts to increase housing, are some of the basic ingredients of a comprehensive social policy and a world development policy. Population is also part of such a policy, but only one of many parts.

The Population Dilemma

This brings us to one of the central controversies of the population dilemma. On one side are the population controllers who believe that population growth is out of control and that the government must use all possible means to lower fertility rates, regardless of the dangers to human freedom or the effects on family life. Dr. Paul Ehrlich, a leader in the population control movement, believes that there are two approaches to the population problem. He describes them as the "birthrate solution," in which we find ways to lower birthrates, and the "death rate solution," in which war, pestilence and famine will bring about a decrease in population. In his book, *The Population Bomb,* Ehrlich writes: "Too many people—that is why we are on the verge of the death rate solution."

Those who see population simply in terms of crisis, who apply "the population explosion" model to every nation and culture, generally end up recommending the curtailment of population increase by any and all methods available. This includes the use of abortion and sterilization as means of population control, and the assignment of a large measure of power to government. For instance, the Commission on Population Growth and the American Future [see "Population Commission Report," in this section, above] assumed that nothing beneficial would result from increased population growth in the United States, and then urged that every possible means be used to eliminate unwanted children. The Commission also proposed the two-child family as the ideal.

The Commission went on to recommend the removal of all legal restrictions on abortion and sterilization. The human rights of the child prior to birth were dismissed, and the Commission did not deal with the effects of easily available sterilization for teenagers without parental consent. Implicit in the Commission report was the assumption that lowering population growth was such a desirable social goal that value questions of human rights, family life and human freedom would have to give way to pragmatic decision-making. Similar thinking was in evidence throughout the United States Supreme Court's opinions on abortion laws. Yet, the clear and proven fact in every nation that has used abortion as a means of population control is that "liberal" abortion is counterproductive as far as family planning and population planning are concerned. The experience of the Eastern European nations is a good example. Family planning programs are generally ineffective, resulting in gaps in the age-structure and extraordinarily low birthrates.

Moreover, when statistical calculations become the determining factor, subtle coercion is exercised on the poorest members of the society. Commitments to social justice and human freedom are lost sight of. The poor and minority groups have spoken strongly and often of this concern in the United States.

On the other side of the controversy are the developmentalists who approach social problems that result in dehumanized living conditions—i.e., economic, governmental, developmental problems—with the conviction that as people begin to experience development and progress, they will in fact slow population growth. Though no one can explain exactly why this is so, it is an historically proven fact.

The National Academy of Sciences, in a 1971 *Report on Rapid Population Growth,* provides a moderate statement of this position:

> The belief is widespread that uncontrolled population growth is leading to catastrophe. It is possible, however, to take a different view, based on what we know about the history of human populations and on the behavior of many people at the present time—a view that social invention will lead to a deliberate limitation of fertility by individual couples.

Another fact to keep in mind is that predictions about the future are difficult and tenuous. To compare available resources with per capita consumption rates is fairly simple. And it is easy and tempting to project increased demands of a growing population against finite supplies of particular resources. But consumption rates can change, and knowledge of existing natural resources is far from accurate.

Moreover, this type of analysis overlooks man's ability

to manipulate resources, the discovery of new resources or the manufacture of synthetic materials that replace older materials, and the ability of mankind to live with some restraints on the use of scarce natural resources.

The United Nations has designated 1974 as UN Population Year. During 1974 there will be a series of international conferences focusing on population. Every nation is being urged to conduct massive educational programs to alert people to the questions related to population growth and distribution. But the UN is not merely urging information and education. Rather, the UN hopes that the visibility given to population questions will lead governments to develop population policies that will determine future population trends. And UN planners also hope that a heightened awareness in individual nations will result in international or global policies that will affect the planet and future generations for centuries to come. We turn now to population policy.

Population Policy

As indicated previously, there are different approaches to the population question. Correspondingly, there are also different perspectives on population policy. Consider the following:

1. "Couples have a basic human right to decide freely and responsibly on the number and spacing of their children and a right to adequate education and information in this respect. . . ." (Resolution of UN International Conference on Human Rights, May 12, 1968)

2. "Economic and social development is an essential element of and prerequisite to an effective population policy." (Res. 1672 of UN Economic and Social Council, June 2, 1972)

3. "There are many other problems of quality in American life. Thus alongside the challenges of population growth and distribution is the challenge of population policy. *The goal of all population policy must be to make better the life that is actually lived.* [Emphasis added by author] (Commission on Population Growth and the American Future, Final Report, March 10, 1972.)

4. "If parenthood is a right, population control is impossible. If parenthood is only a privilege, and if parents see themselves as trustees of the germ plasm and guardians of the rights of future generations, then there is hope for mankind." (Garrett Hardin, *Science,* July 31, 1970.)

The Catholic Bishops of the world stated at the Second Vatican Council that "Governments undoubtedly have rights and duties, within the limits of their proper competency, regarding the population problem in their respective countries. . . ." These rights and duties of governments are based on moral principles respecting the dignity of man, the right of married couples to determine the size of the family and the frequency of births, and a recognition of man's spiritual nature. Purely pragmatic attempts to reduce birthrates can easily violate human dignity, and are unlikely to prove effective over a long period of time. A population policy, then, must be one aspect of a larger social policy that is comprehensive, positive and supportive of family life. As the National Academy of Science report puts it: "In drawing up the government budget, setting priorities, allocating administrative manpower and deciding on alternative uses of resources, fertility policies should be considered in connection with other human resource policies."

The Church is aware of the efforts of various governments to establish population policies. However, the Church contributes to the overall discussion of population by constantly focusing attention on the dignity of man as a child of God and a member of human society. The following propositions can be read as a summary of principles basic to the establishment of morally acceptable population policies:

1. Within the limits of their own competence, government officials have rights and duties with regard to the population problems of their own nations—for instance, in the matter of social legislation as it affects families, of migration to cities, of information relative to the conditions

and needs of the nation. (Vatican Council II, *Constitution on the Church in the Modern World,* #87)

2. Decisions about family size and frequency of births belong to the parents and cannot be left to public authorities. (Vatican Council II, *Constitution on the Church in the Modern World,* #50, #87; Paul VI, *On the Development of Peoples,* #37) Such decisions depend on a rightly formed conscience which "respects the divine law and takes into consideration the circumstances of the place and the time." (Vatican Council II, *Constitution on the Church in the Modern World,* #87) In forming their conscience, parents should "take into account their responsibilities towards God, themselves, the children they have already brought into the world and the community to which they belong." (*On the Development of Peoples,* #37)

3. Public authorities can provide information and recommend certain policies, provided these are in conformity with moral law and respect the rightful freedom of married couples. (Vatican Council II, *Constitution on the Church in the Modern World,* #87; *On the Development of Peoples,* #37; Paul VI, *Humanae Vitae,* #23) In order to safeguard the autonomy of the family and the personal freedom of parents, government suasion should be limited to what is necessary to protect the common good.

4. Men should be informed of scientific advances of methods of family planning "whose safety has been well proven and whose harmony with the moral order has been ascertained." (Vatican Council II, *Constitution on the Church in the Modern World,* #87)

5. "Abortion, directly willed and procured, even if for therapeutic reasons, is to be absolutely excluded as a licit means of regulating births." (*Humanae Vitae,* #14)

In a pluralistic society, any attempts to establish a population policy based on man's dignity and fully responsive to human needs, should include the following goals:

1. A population policy should sustain adequate population growth and distribution.

2. A population policy should be part of a larger policy of social development. It should look to the development of sufficient resources to service the existing population and its projected increase. Each step the government takes in urging people to meet demographic goals should be paralleled by efforts to improve social conditions and extend a full range of social opportunities—jobs, housing, health care, education—to all citizens.

3. A population policy must support the family unit, enabling the family to pursue its own goals while fulfilling responsibilities to the overall society.

4. A population policy should preserve adequate *freedom* for the individual couple to bear and support the number of children they desire. It is the positive duty of government to help bring about conditions that will relieve pressures on couples to limit family size.

5. When a population policy involves education and assistance in family planning, it should include only those means of family planning that are in accord with the moral law and the dignity of man. Acceptance of family planning assistance should be voluntary, with legal prohibition of coercion, particularly for the poor who are often considered the target of family planning programs.

6. Abortion, which violates the right to life of the unborn child, should be excluded as a method of population control.

7. Research into all phases of the family life-cycle and the effects of social trends on the family should be part of a population policy. There should also be funding for demographic research and for the scientific work that will lead to the development of safe and morally acceptable methods of family planning.

8. A population policy should provide a full range of prenatal, maternal health and pediatric services, and nutritional care.

9. In order to benefit families, a population policy may also include ancillary services such as education in human sexuality and in marriage and family living, and premarriage and marriage counseling.

The development of population policies at the national and international levels will achieve much public attention and discussion during the remainder of the present decade. The Church should inject the moral perspective and a concern for human dignity into the public discussion. Failure to do so may result in policies that are materialistic, utilitarian and pragmatic, and therefore contrary to the dignity of man. Moreover, cautious initiation and continued reexamination of a population policy are necessary, so that solutions to ad hoc problems, regardless of the likelihood of short-range effectiveness, may be measured also in terms of long-range harmful effects.

At best, population planning is risky and uncertain because of unknown factors and our inability to accurately project future trends for more than a few decades. If the policies of the nation are directed toward decreasing the birthrate at any cost—and by any means—the emphasis is placed on the abstract demographic ideal, and the value of the life of an individual person takes second place. If on the other hand, we emphasize the value of the person and the sanctity of human life, we create incentives to improve the circumstances of human living—i.e., the human environment—and to protect human life at every point of existence. Responsible parenthood then becomes a realistic guideline for the individual couple who must consider the size of the family and the frequency of births in the context of responsibilities to God, to themselves and their present family, and to society at large.

CONTRACEPTION FOR TEENAGERS? [6]

As a society, we have been reluctant to acknowledge that there is a considerable amount of sexual activity among unmarried young people. The national study which disclosed that 27 percent of unmarried girls fifteen to nineteen years old had had sexual relations, further revealed that girls have a considerable acquaintance with contraceptive methods; over 95 percent of all girls fifteen to nineteen, for example, know about the pill. Contraceptive practice, however, contrasts sharply with this picture. Although many young women who have had intercourse have used a contraceptive at some time, this age group is characterized by a great deal of "chance taking." The majority of these young women have either never used or, at best, have sometimes used birth control methods.

We deplore the various consequences of teenage pregnancy, including the . . . report from New York that teenagers account for about one quarter of the abortions performed. . . . Adolescent pregnancy offers a generally bleak picture of serious physical, psychological, and social implications for the teenager and the child. Once a teenager becomes pregnant, her chances of enjoying a rewarding, satisfying life are diminished. Pregnancy is the number one cause for school dropout among females in the United States. The psychological effects of adolescent pregnancy are indicated by a . . . study that estimated that teenage mothers have a suicide attempt rate ten times that of the general population.

The Commission [on Population Growth and the American Future] is not addressing the moral questions involved in teenage sexual behavior. However, we are concerned with the complex issue of teenage pregnancy. Therefore, the Commission believes that young people must be given access to contraceptive information and services.

[6] From *Population and the American Future: The Report of the Commission on Population Growth and the American Future.* Supt. of Docs. Washington, D.C. 20402. '72. p 109.

Recommendation

Toward the goal of reducing unwanted pregnancies and childbearing among the young, the Commission recommends that birth control information and services be made available to teenagers in appropriate facilities sensitive to their needs and concerns.

The Commission recognizes that the availability of contraceptive services alone is insufficient. It has . . . been reported that among teenagers, the single most important reason given for not using contraceptives was the belief that, for various reasons, they could not become pregnant. Our survey reveals that nearly two thirds of our citizens are in favor of high schools offering information on ways to avoid pregnancy.

Young people whose family-building years lie in the future and whose options will depend on their understanding of fertility control and services available to them, must have accurate information about these matters.

Implementation of Program

The Commission therefore recommends the development and implementation of an adequately financed program to develop appropriate family planning materials, to conduct training courses for teachers and school administrators, and to assist states and local communities in integrating information about family planning into school courses such as hygiene and sex education.

TEENAGE SEXUALITY AND FAMILY PLANNING SERVICES TO MINORS [7]

Our society has neglected to deal responsibly with the sexuality of its teenagers.

Accordingly, the Planned Parenthood Federation of America strongly endorses The Commission on Population

---

[7] *Teenage Sexuality and Family Planning Services to Minors,* [Statement] *Adopted by the Membership, October 26, 1972.* Planned Parenthood Federation of America. 810 Seventh Ave. New York 10019. '72.

Growth and the American Future's recommendation on services to minors by adopting the following policy statement:

Reality today is that services responsive to health and welfare needs, most critically in the area of sexuality and fertility, continue to be denied to minors on the basis of their age alone. We believe that this denial constitutes an infringement of their rights as individuals. We believe that all medical services should be rendered according to individual needs and ability to comprehend and cope with the type of care requested and indicated, and on this basis only. Services to minors should be provided on the basis of their need and request for such services and on their own consent alone.

Furthermore, the Federation affirms the belief that an important part of providing complete fertility control services to minors is the development of knowledge and understanding among minors of their sexuality.

SEX EDUCATION [8]

There has never been as great a need for good sex education in the schools of America as there is today. And yet only a small fraction of our youngsters are getting any organized sex education at all in school, and of those schools that have a program, only a few provide one adequate to prepare boys and girls to make responsible choices in difficult situations. Some schools and school systems have issued broad statements favoring "family life education," or "health education," or "human relations," but most of these—including the schools of my own city, Philadelphia—do not implement the statements by organizing real classes, taught by well-trained teachers, based on the problems the kids face and answering the questions they want to ask and need to be able to discuss and consider.

Today, for better or worse, there are few boys or girls

[8] From "What Do You Want Your Children to Learn About Sex?" by Eric W. Johnson, vice principal, Germantown Friends School, Philadelphia. *Parents' Magazine.* 47:40-1+. Ap. '72. Reprinted by permission.

ten years old or older who are truly innocent of some of the facts of sex and of many aspects of sexual behavior. TV, radio, phonograph records, magazines, movies, and advertising have taken away innocence. But the end of innocence is not the same thing as the beginning of wisdom. The knowledge of our boys and girls comes too often from descriptions and pictures of sexual behavior that are mostly fantasy; it is based on values that overemphasize pure physical sensation; therefore, it puts sex out of proportion with the rest of life. I feel that the foundation for responsible decisions in the field of sex, as in any field, is full knowledge placed in good perspective. It seems to me that the half-truths and rumors so easily picked up by boys and girls—and not a few adults—need to be countered by complete information, plainly told.

We need not fear that the knowledge presented in a sound program will lead to experimentation and trouble. Those who get into trouble are not generally those who are truly and fully informed.

Because of our confusion and ignorance, problems involving sex are found at every level of our society: divorce rates are high; there is vast unhappiness within many marriages; too many teenagers are getting married, often because of premarital pregnancy, and the odds are high against the success of such marriages; we have over a million and a half new cases of venereal disease each year, many among the young; more than a third of a million babies are born out of wedlock each year.

If there is such a need for sex education, why do people object to it? I believe that the objections are not as widely held as some of us think. Public opinion polls show that more than two thirds of the respondents favor sex education in the schools. It is approved by many national organizations, including the American Academy of Pediatrics, the American College of Obstetricians and Gynecologists, the American Medical Association, the National Association for Mental Health, the National Congress of Parents and Teachers, the National Council of Churches, the National Education Association, the White House Conference on Children and Youth, the Synagogue Council of America, and the United States Catholic Conference.

But there are those who object. Many of them, I know from experience, are people who have been misled by fear-groups who have spread rumors and lies about what supposedly goes on in sex education classes. These groups are led by people whose true aim often seems to be to use our fears of the misuse of sex to undermine good established programs and to exert influence over entire school systems for purposes which have little to do with concern about sex. Fortunately, these organized attacks are now on the wane, and, despite the harm they have done, they have had some good effect by causing educators to examine even more carefully their objectives and practices and to take more time to involve the public fully in the development of their plans.

There is not space in an article like this to present fully what should go into a sex education program. Let me just suggest some of the essentials. First, of course, are the biological facts of sex and reproduction—even though a sex education program is not as much biology as it is anthropology, sociology, human relations, and discussions of the conduct of life. The program should teach the facts of birth control and family planning—these are facts that are needed even by people who are religiously opposed to birth control, for if people don't know the facts, they will accept rumor and half-truth, often with tragic results. We should teach, also, the differences in sexual behavior in animals and human beings—that the sexual behavior of animals is largely instinctive, but the sexual behavior of human beings is mostly learned. We should teach and discuss the differences between men and women, not just the biological differences but the differences in sexual roles, in sexual response, in personality, and in what society expects. We should teach, in addition, the facts about masturbation; we should teach such facts as are known about homosexuality, and we should discuss the rights and problems of people with homosexual preferences. We should teach the facts about venereal disease, to help young people protect themselves against this rapidly growing health problem. We should teach, again largely through discussion, the results, good and bad, of sexual intercourse and the steps that lead up to it; the place of sex in family life; the place of sex in the social life of teenagers. Through discussion, we should help each youngster to recognize that the feelings of others often are not the same as his; we should help students to put themselves in the place of other people.

When should all this be taught? parents ask. My belief is that the organized, definitely scheduled sex education program should not begin until about grade five, when the boys and girls are about ten years old. From kindergarten through grade four, I think that the best approach for those teachers who feel easy and comfortable about it and have had some preparation and training is to take advantage of any opportunities that arise naturally to answer questions and allow the children to talk things over. I mean such opportunities as when a child reports that his mother is having a baby and the children want to know about it: how did it get started? how does it get born? and so on. Certainly, it is best for the teacher to answer the questions that are asked rather than avoid them. The answers should be simple and factual and not go beyond the question and the discussion that naturally follows—in other words, a question about how babies get started should not lead into a full-scale lecture on sexual intercourse. . . .

From fifth grade on, I believe, schools should continue the informal, spontaneous sex education, but from here on it should be accompanied by organized, planned units, perhaps lasting a month or six weeks and taking place every other year or so. In these units, the biology of reproduction should be covered, and increasingly, as the students move toward graduation, questions of sex and human relations and what it means to be a man or woman in our society should be discussed. Ideally, by the time the boys and girls are feeling the pressures and desires to engage in sexual activity, they will have discussed and thought through its consequences, so that when they are ready to establish families of their own, they will have considered what goes into a good family life, and they will have been provided, as SIECUS (the Sex Education and Information Council of the U.S.) puts it, with "enough knowledge about the misuse and aberrations of sex to enable them to protect themselves against exploitation and against injury to their physical and mental health." They will have been stimulated "to work for a society in which such evils as prostitution and illegitimacy, archaic sex laws, irrational fears of sex, and sexual exploitation are non-existent." (I would add to the list of evils, that of world overpopulation.)

SCHOOL SEX EDUCATION OPPOSED [9]

CBE [the Council for Basic Education] does not take an absolutist position about sex education in the schools, one way or the other. Reliable knowledge about sex is necessary for young people and conceivably some schools are better equipped than some parents to transmit that knowledge (although we wouldn't want to press the point too far). If the schools are to take on this additional task we recommend . . . [a] cautious approach. . . . We continue to have doubts about some current efforts, especially those that turn sex education into a crusade.

These remarks are prompted by an interview with Dr. Mary Calderone which appeared . . . [in 1968] in *Family Weekly*, a reprint of which was . . . sent to us by the Sex Information and Education Council of the U.S. (SIECUS), the organization in which Dr. Calderone is the moving spirit. Dr. Calderone's good intentions are obvious but we

[9] From "Further Doubts About Sex Education." *Bulletin of the Council for Basic Education*. 13:8-9. Ja. '69. Reprinted by permission.

find some of her ideas confusing and vague. We are confused because we are not at all sure what she wants the schools to teach. Near the beginning of the interview she states that "the simple facts of reproduction . . . are not sex education really . . ." but several questions later she talks about acquiring the physiology of reproduction in school courses and expresses hope that parents will talk early about reproduction and share with their children a series of slides called "How Babies Are Made." She doesn't think that knowledge of venereal diseases is a part of sex education (she assigns that to "communicable-disease education") but apparently would include discussion of abortion. Says she: "To me, there is no controversial subject in sex. Anything that exists is here, and, therefore, we must explore it, understand it, and learn as much as we can about it." *Anything?* At what grade level do we expect young people to "understand" shoe-fetishism? And when do we "explore" bestiality or any of the other aberrations that exist and therefore "must" be explored?

If Dr. Calderone is confusing on the specifics of sex education she is also vague in describing the general nature of the subject. It's all very well to say, as she does, that sex education isn't talk about sex techniques but about "what it is to be a man and what it is to be a woman," but what, actually, does such a statement mean? Again, she can talk about preparing children "to live sexually in today's world" and about giving children what they need "to help them learn how to manage their perfectly normal sexual needs," but such talk seems to us to be mostly fine mist. One is sometimes tempted to respond to the language of the sex education buff with an irreverent quip, but it must be borne in mind that sex educators are a solemn group, not naturally receptive to humor.

When it comes to the question of who is qualified to teach sex education we find Dr. Calderone particularly unsatisfactory. It's no problem, apparently, as long as the teacher relates honestly to young people. There is nothing "so abstruse about human sexual behavior that any teacher could not teach it" and she suggests that "summer courses in the universities" will take care of the teacher training. On the other hand, she thinks that most parents are not qualified to judge the content of courses, nor are doctors, except to judge the accuracy of the biology and physiology involved. A different kind of judgment is required for "the emotional and behavioral content," a judgment that teachers, apparently, can easily pick up in summer school, while such judgment continues to elude parents.

Perhaps we make too much of the interview with Dr. Calderone, but because SIECUS at the present time seems to be the organizational focus for selling sex education to the schools we think it useful to make note of her comments. As we have said before . . . , we frankly do not know if sex education is reducible to courses, except for the biological facts. As we have also said before, perhaps true sex education is encompassed in art and literature and in ethics, where man is considered as a whole human being. Any wisdom gleaned by students from these studies will carry over into all aspects of their lives, including their sexuality. We confess to being bothered not only by the fuzzy goals of SIECUS but by what seems to us to be a tendency to make a mystique of sex education.

IV. QUESTIONS OF DISCRIMINATION

EDITOR'S INTRODUCTION

In this fourth section, special problems affecting two minority groups are considered—the blacks and the aged. While some of the more militant male leaders in the black community have called for rapid increases in the black population to increase blacks' political power, this position has not been generally supported by the black women who would have to bear the children. Representative Shirley Chisholm of New York, as a black leader and a black woman, comes out for making contraception available to black women. Furthermore, a male-dominated organization, the National Association for the Advancement of Colored People, speaking through Roy Wilkins, supports family planning. In contrast, the Rev. Jesse Jackson argues that economic justice for blacks is more important than family limitation. It may be noted that the demographic facts show that black behavior with regard to family size is much the same as the behavior of whites in the same economic groups.

As for our senior citizens, their numbers are steadily increasing, as are their problems. The concluding article in this section, written by Barbara Isenberg for the *Nation*, gives the details of this increase in numbers and outlines the problems and the growing efforts of older people to attain political power.

BLACK ECONOMIC SOLUTIONS [1]

The nation's preoccupation with multiple crises is evi-

[1] Excerpt entitled "Population Control Is Subordinate to Wealth Control," by Rev. Jesse Jackson, president of People United to Save Humanity, taken from article "Black Perspectives." *In* New York *Times* Supplement "Population: The U.S. Problem, the World Crisis." New York *Times*. Sec 12, p 12. Ap. 30, '72. © 1972 by the Population Crisis Committee. Reprinted by permission.

denced by the description of the population challenge as a population bomb. Yet, if life for us in the 1970s is more problem than possibility, we may well be in danger of losing that race which H. G. Wells described as "education's race with disaster . . ."—the race to create a sound and meaningful civilization.

The alarmist concern for "Zero" population growth is by and large predicated upon Malthusian premises about population growth as over against the ability to meet the needs of that growth. But modern technology increasingly makes Malthus' views obsolete. If there is any issue of human survival, it is one which must be defined on a new terrain, determined in large measure by the entitlement of the have-nots, world-wide and in this nation, to a larger share of the available resources.

In this country, the real issue is not an unmanageable surplus of people but a basic maldistribution of the resources. Over 20 percent of the nation's population, in Dr. Martin Luther King's words "languish on an island of poverty in a vast sea of affluence. . . ."

Another reason for suspecting the stridency of some population control advocates is that, despite reports predicting the inevitability of a big baby boom, reinforced by the spectre of 8.5 million women in prime reproductive years by 1970 and 1 million more by 1975, the baby boom has just not materialized. In fact, some population experts are admitting that, with a population of 200 million today and with the continuation of present trends, the projection of 300 million by the year 2000 may prove too high.

Without becoming simplistic in exploring a very complex problem, I would submit the following reservations which I have about the population control issue:

First, when the more militant of my colleagues refer to the total policy as the initial step to legitimizing genocide, they are considered downright alarmists. Yet the timing of the population issue is a source of some concern. That this issue should surface simultaneously with the emergence of blacks and other nonwhites as a meaningful force in the nation and the world appears more than coincidental.

Black Strength in Numbers

Second, blacks, devoid of economic strength, must seek to deploy skillfully the strength they have in numbers. But a population policy, such as is proposed, may well dilute that strength. There are now fifty locations in this nation where black people are 50 percent or more of the population, and over 200 locations where blacks are now 30 percent or more. This is a power of numbers which blacks cannot afford to think of lightly. . . . Court decisions could mean hundreds of more black public officials at all levels, throughout the South. Thus, just the simple arithmetic of "one man, one vote" could so transform the face of politics in this nation as to make Dr. King's fondest dreams of Selma a fundamental fact of this democracy.

Black Poverty Critical

Third, black people need a vastly larger equity in the resources of this nation. For the poverty, which we must now freight to the political bargaining table, is itself evidence of our vulnerability. Black Americans possess only 2 percent of the total US wealth. Black businesses had receipts in 1969-70 representing .7 of 1 percent of the total business receipts of the nation. Black banks presently control one fiftieth of 1 percent of the banking assets of the nation.

Black economic penury is a critical issue. It spotlights the relevance of our demands for a greater share of the resources while, at the same time, corroborating our central argument that the creation of a more equitable distribution system is of greater priority than population control. Population control is subordinate to wealth control. For a nation which engineered the Berlin airlift and the lift to the moon, the challenge is to wed its resources with its compassion to build a human community.

BLACK WOMEN'S RIGHTS [2]

I have long been and still am an ardent advocate of family planning. I believe that every woman has the right to control her own reproductive process. The decision to have children, when and how many, is one of the most important decisions she will make in her entire lifetime. But too often, for a variety of reasons, she doesn't decide at all; the pregnancy just occurs.

One of the biggest problems is the lack of information about the reproductive process and contraception. Studies have shown that most poor families as well as the American population in general desire a family of two or three children. The poor however have much less access to either good prenatal or postnatal care or information about contraceptive techniques.

The result, limited financial resources are insufficient and the family may sink even deeper into poverty. More than one quarter of all families with four or more children are living in poverty. Their risk of poverty is two-and-a-half times that for families with three children or less.

Another serious and growing problem is illegitimacy. As of 1967 approximately 4.5 million children under the age of 18 in the United States were illegitimate. A recent study by the government of the District of Columbia showed that in 1970 the percentage of illegitimate births had exceeded 40 percent and projected that by 1973 over half the babies in the District will be born out of wedlock. [This estimate proved accurate.—Ed.]

We can't ignore this. These children and this problem are not going to just fade away. We need to be concerned

[2] Excerpt entitled "Given the Opportunity Many Women Will Choose to Have Fewer Children," by Shirley A. Chisholm, member of the United States House of Representatives from New York, taken from article "Black Perspectives." *In* New York *Times* Supplement "Population: The U.S. Problem, the World Crisis." New York *Times*. Sec 12, p 13. Ap. 30, '72. © 1972 by the Population Crisis Committee. Reprinted by permission.

about the quality of these lives—both of the children and of their mothers.

Even though approximately 40 percent of the mothers of the 245,000 babies born illegitimately in the United States every year are women nineteen years old or younger, we still are not making information on birth control available to these young girls. Although many young people seem to be very sophisticated about sex, they, in fact, are frequently lacking in knowledge about the facts of life. By forcing a young girl to have an unwanted child, we are assigning her to society's trash heap. Young, confused, usually without skills or training, she will be cut off from avenues of opportunity.

My own experiences at the community level and other studies done after the introduction of the New York State abortion repeal law confirm the fact that given the opportunity many women will choose to have fewer children.

There are those who either for religious or personal convictions believe that abortion and certain forms of contraception are morally wrong and amount to killing a child; others believe that human life does not start until some time after conception or at birth. I believe that this is a matter of personal conscience which should not be decided by the State. . . .

At the other end of the spectrum are those who advocate sterilization and a limitation on the number of children a family may have, as a solution to the "population problem." While it is true that our population and that of the world is growing at an astounding rate and that we do need to be concerned about the conservation of human resources, forced sterilization or any compulsory directive is an anathema to the human spirit.

It is the suggestion of compulsory birth control regulations that has prompted concern among American blacks about "race genocide." There have been instances when judges have ordered individuals, such as convicted felons, to be sterilized, and there have been suggestions that women be "required" to use contraceptives or have an abortion as a prerequisite to receipt of public assistance. Indeed there are reports that some social workers already imply that those who don't attend family planning seminars will have difficulty with the welfare office.

There is a difference between making information and services available and coercion. It is a very important difference that we must jealously guard and respect. Women should neither be forced into having children they don't want nor restricted from having children they do want.

NAACP FOR FAMILY PLANNING [3]

The National Association for the Advancement of Colored People supports "the dissemination of information and materials concerning family health and family planning to all those who desire it."

In taking this position the NAACP does not ignore the traditional concern of the Association, indeed, the reason for its being, the racial discrimination against minority groups that is so prevalent in all aspects of American life. It recognizes that

the family constitutes the foundation of our society. . . . The general well-being of the family and all the services that affect it— are of paramount concern to this Association. It is further recognized that, although numerous health and welfare benefits are available, both overt and subtle forms of discrimination are practiced in the rendition of these services to minority groups.

Special emphasis is placed upon the welfare system and the myths which have been given wide currency in order, in part, to "justify" racial discrimination. There is, however, no ambiguity in the NAACP approach to the significant, but highly emotional, topic of family planning. The Asso-

[3] Excerpt entitled "Minority Groups Shall Not Be Denied Access to Family Planning," by Roy Wilkins, executive director, National Association for the Advancement of Colored People, taken from article "Black Perspectives." In New York *Times* Supplement "Population: The U.S. Problem, the World Crisis." New York *Times*. Sec 12, p 13. Ap. 30, '72. © 1972 by the Population Crisis Committee. Reprinted by permission.

ciation supports the dissemination of "information and materials" for those who wish it.

The NAACP does not purport to be a crusader for family planning. That is the task of those organizations specifically designed and equipped to render the services where requested. However, the NAACP does not believe that obstacles should be placed in the way of the dissemination of information on the subject.

There can be no question that family size beyond the capacities of available income or of health and educational resources, constitutes a genuine problem. . . .

The basic determination of the NAACP is that minority group families, who must wrestle with myriad manifestations of racial discrimination, shall not be denied access to family planning help by reason of their racial and economic deprivations.

NEEDED: SENIOR POWER [4]

Old age, it seems, is something the young do not think about, the middle-aged do not like to think about, and the elderly think about all the time. Those of us still under sixty-five talk of old age as if it were something that happens to others, not to us. But the years pass quickly.

Perhaps the reason Americans choose not to think about aging is that in America today it is a dismal thought. The majority of today's elderly are poor; most feel useless, afraid and lonely. And while much is being done to ameliorate that situation, it is too little and comes too late for those already old. The numbers and problems of old people have outdistanced the country's present capacity to deal with them.

Forty years ago, the elderly were 5 per cent of the population; today they are 10 per cent. In the United States today, 21 million people are sixty-five or older, and the esti-

⁴ From "Senior Power: Aging in America," by Barbara Isenberg, staff reporter for the *Wall Street Journal* in Los Angeles. *Nation.* 216:626-8. My. 14. '73. © 1973 by The Nation Associates, Inc. Reprinted with permission.

mates are for 25 million by 1985 and 29 million by the year 2000. Every day more than 4,000 people turn sixty-five, and every day some 3,000 over sixty-five die; that leaves a net increase of more than 1,000 new elderly daily.

Half of the older population is seventy-three or older, and, because of improvements in medical care, that portion of the elderly population is growing even faster than the rest—Social Security is paying benefits to more than 6,500 centenarians.

The greatest problem for most aged people is money. A substantial number of the elderly have incomes averaging less than $75 a week. Many live on far less, particularly the very old whose life spans have outlasted their resources. While only 10 per cent of the population, the elderly represent 20 per cent of the poor. Senator Frank Church (chairman of the Senate Special Committee on Aging, found . . . [in 1972] that 100,000 more elderly people were living in poverty than had been doing so just two years before.

While many of the elderly have always been poor, others are newly poor, having been booted by society into mandatory retirement without adequate reserves. Productive all their lives, they find in retirement not tranquility but trauma: how will they survive as inflation eats at fixed incomes and rising property taxes threaten mortgage-free homes, often the only asset they have left?

Only 16 per cent of the elderly are still in the work force, and preliminary data indicate[d] that the percentage . . . [was] falling in 1973. Even the wealthier aged live for the most part on fixed incomes, and they, too, are penalized by inflation they can neither control nor enjoy. While other age groups have options—they can switch jobs, strike, threaten work stoppage—the retired have no such recourse.

Simone de Beauvoir, in *The Coming of Age,* refers to retirement as "the most loathsome word in the language," and most retired people would agree with her. Even the well-to-do are hard-pressed to find meaning in retirement; Ralph Nader's Retired Professional Action Group received seven hundred applications from retired professionals for its twelve voluntary positions.

In a . . . survey on old age, the Los Angeles *Times* found that older women associated it with loneliness, older men associated it with poverty, and youth associated it with death. Each group feared it, yet each feared it only in part. However, old age has all those parts—poverty, loneliness, the prospect of death—plus what is probably the worst part of all: uselessness. A feeling of being shelved by a society which no longer needs you, although you still need that society. . . .

Fortunately, however, the situation is not static. At this time when the nature of the elderly population is changing in size, activity and awareness, society is stretching its institutions to offer more alternatives to the elderly and others. It appears that in the future the aged should know greater choice than did their predecessors.

A new breed of the vocal elderly is egging on the more passive in their age group. As recently as ten years ago, the aged were poorly organized, without political voice, and doing little to help themselves; they waited for an uninterested society to notice them. But since society did not notice and the problems showed no signs of going away, the elderly turned to protest and organization to help themselves.

Perhaps six million old people . . . [belonged in 1973] to senior organizations on either the local or national level—compared to 250,000 a decade [before]—and a good many of these groups are more than social clubs. Across the country, the aged are winning battles ranging from discounted bus fares to property tax relief.

"Senior power" has become a political force to be reckoned with. The aged represent some 15 per cent of the electorate, and they vote with great regularity. Few politicians choose to ignore what some pundit once dubbed "the crutch, cane and Cadillac" vote.

Everyone knows of the continual boosts in Social Security. In addition, the elderly have successfully led investigations to close down nursing homes in Illinois, demonstrated and succeeded in halting Medicaid cuts in New York, and organized sit-ins which produced needed traffic lights at intersections in Michigan. They have asked for and received discounted bus fares in more than fifty cities and are now trying to obtain similar discounts on utility bills. Senior citizens have learned that protest is no longer the prerogative of the young.

Meanwhile, the government and other institutions have stepped up both funds and manpower for research on gerontology. Most of this money appears to be focused on understanding the aging process and on stretching out the life span, but it is important that we not only prolong life but enrich it. For many people, sixty-five years of coping with life feels like one hundred years.

Many of the trials of old age can certainly be softened and some can be eliminated through both a reordering of priorities by society and better planning by the individual. In many cases, such social change would help not only the elderly but other age groups as well.

Senior groups like the National Council of Senior Citizens and the Retired Teachers Association/American Association of Retired Persons, both based in Washington, have long urged reform in property taxes, Social Security and private pensions, and legislation on these issues is continually under study in Congress. . . .

The aged who have private pensions often find upon retirement that they receive far fewer benefits than they had counted on. And Social Security payments, despite many increases, are still not enough for those who live on them exclusively. In addition, the restriction on earned income for those receiving Social Security discourages work which provides emotional as well as material rewards. Old-age assistance in many states is so enmeshed in bureaucratic tangles and often so demeaning that more than half the aged nationally eligible do not even apply.

Property taxes could be restructured in order to benefit not just the elderly but their children as well. Nearly two thirds of the aged own their own homes, and property taxes have more than doubled in the past ten years. While more than two dozen states, including California, offer seniors some form of property tax relief, such efforts are still only scratching the surface.

Former Secretary of Health, Education, and Welfare, Wilbur Cohen has called the property tax the major discontent of senior citizens, and it is often the elderly who vote to defeat school bond issues. The federal government currently pays a small part of elementary and secondary education costs, and greater federal funding of public education might lead to lower property taxes. . . .

Health, too, is an intergenerational problem. A form of national health insurance—extending Medicare-type programs to all age levels—will probably be enacted in the next decade or so, and it will greatly improve on Medicare. While it was one of the greatest victories of the aged, Medicare still pays only part of an old person's medical bills. And not everyone waits to get sick until he's sixty-five. With preventive medicine becoming more and more popular, it seems we might soon accept Wilbur Cohen's recommendation that we start taking care of the aged's health when they're born, not when they're sixty-five. . . .

The aged often pay disproportionate amounts of their income for rent. Too many of them live in central-city neighborhoods from which the younger and more affluent have moved on, and where high crime rates are often the price of low rents. In Los Angeles, as elsewhere, urban renewal projects have pushed skid rows into low-rent areas heavily populated by the elderly.

Yet even if the economic and health problems of the elderly were resolved, there would still remain a multitude of social and psychological adjustments. In this area, too, changes are occurring. One is the retirement community. While limited to the more affluent elderly, such communities reverse the situation outside their gates; here, the elderly shove aside the rest of society. At Sun City, Arizona, no one under fifty may buy a house; and no one with school-age children may live there. Some communities, like Rossmoor Corporation's Leisure World at Laguna Hills, even have high walls and security guards who allow admittance only by passes.

While retirement communities are often depicted as segregated lands where the old go to die, they are in fact what their residents make of them. For many aged, such communities offer safe and secure places in which to enjoy activities and friends in their later years; while for others, they are simply well-manicured way stations to the cemetery.

But the aged who give up life would be equally discontent in Sun City or a central city hotel room. Furthermore, my talks with elderly around the country indicate the unadjusted were generally also unhappy, passive or uninvolved when they were younger. People don't undergo radical personality changes the day they turn sixty-five; most of them were basically the same people at thirty, forty or fifty. But problems do compound with the years, and if we can't cope with life when we are young, it will be that much more difficult to cope with it when our options decrease with age. . . .

For people in the work force, experts on aging have long advocated that work be distributed in better fashion throughout the life span so that retirement is not arbitrary but voluntary. Jack Ossofsky, executive director of the National Council on Aging in Washington, argues that while we do need to make space for young people in the work force, there must be a more efficient way to do so than by pushing the elderly out.

Programs run by the National Council on Aging have found that elderly workers can learn new skills well, show less absenteeism, and have fewer accidents. Because they know the ropes, they also show no discernible drop in productivity. Similarly, the United Auto Workers more than a decade ago launched a senior citizen group, with the idea that the union shouldn't discard retirees but rather use their experience and wisdom to guide the young who replace them. . . .

But the most urgent change required of our society is one of attitude. We must end what Washington, D.C., psychiatrist and specialist on aging Dr. Robert N. Butler calls "ageism"—discrimination because of age—for those who deny the aged ultimately deny themselves. Dr. Butler reminds us, "We don't all grow black or Chinese, but we all do grow old."

V. SOCIAL AND ECONOMIC PROBLEMS

EDITOR'S INTRODUCTION

In this final section, some social and economic effects of changing population patterns are detailed. First comes a report from *Newsweek* on the reaction in Vermont to an "invasion" by persons from other states. Many in Vermont are challenging what until recently was an article of faith in America—that growth is good. They see the newcomers mainly as persons bringing problems with them. There follows an article by David A. Andelman, taken from the New York *Times,* analyzing the problems caused by population imbalance in suburban areas around New York City. While some school districts are crowded and are contemplating building more classrooms, others find themselves with empty seats in classrooms. Unbalanced population patterns and difficulties in planning have produced these undesirable results.

In a study of age and crime in Washington, D.C., Lawrence Feinberg, writing in the Washington *Post,* reports on the rapid rise in Washington crime rates (partly caused by an equally rapid rise in the fifteen- to twenty-four-year-old age group, the most prone to crime) and on the increase in the number of single women living alone—a group likely to be victims of criminal attack.

What may be the results of slower population growth are laid out in a *U.S. News & World Report* article which draws a picture of an America with an older population, causing a shift in public expenditures—for instance, less demand for schools and more for health care and pensions—and altered markets, with youth markets contracting and service- and luxury-markets expected to grow. More women, too, are seeking careers outside the home. Furthermore, per capita income is expected to rise more quickly with slower population growth.

In conclusion, in a *Forbes* article, the effect of slowed population growth on business is examined. More disposable income for American families is forecast, income that can be spent for such things as travel, entertainment, second houses, and gourmet foods instead of necessities. With fewer children per family, condominiums are booming in popularity, and this is likely to affect the furniture market, calling for less but better quality furniture. Some firms have already begun to adapt their products and marketing to this emerging situation; others are doing little or nothing. Those who make intelligent and demographically sound plans are likely to be the most successful.

VERMONT AGAINST NEWCOMERS [1]

A decade ago, more cows than people lived in the State of Vermont. Most "woodchucks," as native Vermonters are called, cheered in 1963 when the balance finally turned in favor of humans and for some time thereafter the steadily swelling influx of tourists, second-home buyers and other urban escapees seemed to bode the state nothing but good. Now, however, growing numbers of Vermonters are beginning to wish that all those non-Yankees would simply stay home. "Vermont ain't Vermont any more," complains Theron Boyd, a seventy-year-old farmer. "Folks used to come here because it was different. Now they're trying to make it look like every other state. That's the darn of it."

The invasion from out-of-state has already brought radical change to Vermont. Land prices are soaring, particularly in the southern counties, where an acre that sold for $15 in the 1950s can fetch $1,000 today. Few woodchucks can afford those prices. "There's resentment against the peo-

[1] Article "Non-Yankee Stay Home!" *Newsweek*. 80:86. Jl. 10, '72. Copyright Newsweek, Inc. 1972, reprinted by permission.

ple who are coming in and buying the land that Vermonters have been saving up for," reports Peter Martin, an aide to Governor Deane C. Davis. There's also resentment over the fact that resorts and second-home colonies are blotting out the picturesque landscape in some areas and contributing to air and water pollution. This "recreational pollution" has become so severe that last month the state Board of Health warned that boating and swimming might have to be banned on several major lakes unless the towns that use them for drinking water find other sources of supply.

Thus beleaguered, Vermonters have begun to fight the onslaught of outsiders and many are advocating surprisingly drastic measures. In a statewide poll last year, 42 per cent of the people questioned favored closing Vermont to immigrants from out-of-state and a white paper currently circulating around the state office building in Montpelier proposes a future limit on the state population. Last spring [1972], the Vermont legislature voted to cut back the funds that supported the state's tourist offices in New York and Montreal. Most important of all, Vermont's rock-ribbed Republicans are beginning to institute strict controls over the use of land. Some towns are adopting tough zoning laws to restrict developers and the state government is expected to announce new land-use guidelines this month.

Specter

At one point, a fair number of Vermonters feared that they were going to be overrun by hordes of hippies. Their fears may have been fanned when two Yale Law School students wrote an article proposing that counter-culturists simply take over a small state, such as Vermont. More recently, New York journalist Richard Pollak, writing in *Playboy*, suggested that women's liberationists might turn Bennington County into Steinem County, and that triumphant Yippies could rename Windsor County in honor of Abbie Hoffman. The article prompted one horrified reader to raise the specter that Vermont was about "to be 'liberated' by long-haired, grass-blowing freaks seeking *lebens-raum*."

In sober fact, however, native Vermonters seem to get on surprisingly well with the more hardworking inhabitants of the state's 250 communes (which so far show no sign of taking over anything). . . . [In 1971] one rural town elected a young communard to head its municipal finance committee and Peter Martin reports that "we almost fell off our chairs in the Statehouse when one of the old woodchuck legislators tried to help a long-haired youth get a state grant for some work he's doing." "There's a great sense of the work ethic here," says one twenty-eight-year-old urban dropout who has turned to farming in Vermont. "But you really have to earn the respect of the old-timers; we've lived here full-time for a year and it's only now that we're getting to know our neighbors."

Shock

At bottom, in fact, it is the "straight" settlers that give Vermont the most trouble. In addition to retired people and owners of vacation homes, the state has attracted many middle-class immigrants who hope to find work in Vermont. "It's shocking to us to see professional people come up here without jobs," says Roland Loveless, head of the state's Development and Community Affairs agency. "We're not sure what's going to become of them." Even vacation homes may pose a threat. "What's going to happen to those so-called second homes?" asks state planning director Benjamin Partridge "I'll tell you: Mom and the kids will stay in the country while Dad works in the city. You can imagine the expensive new services that will be demanded of small towns—new schools, sewage and utilities, more police and fire protection. And it's already happening."

The vacation-home developments are also criticized by many woodchucks for poor design. "You couldn't believe those horrible developments," says Partridge. "Some of the first ones had individual septic tanks on less than half an acre; the residents were . . . dumping sewage on each other. And around those ski-lodge developments were all sorts of ugly restaurants and garish nightclubs. It woke us up, all right."

One of the biggest developments is Quechee Lakes, a six-thousand-acre complex near White River Junction. Over the next decade, at least two thousand houses and five hundred condominiums will be erected around private golf and ski facilities. Many of the current inhabitants of the area are dismayed by the vast undertaking. And . . . [in May 1972] the citizens of neighboring Pomfret took steps to keep the development from spreading into their town. They drew up a zoning code that prohibits the sale of land in parcels smaller than two acres or the sale of more than two commercially built houses every two years on a single piece of property. "We're not trying to stop progress," contends Pomfret selectwoman Dorothy Moore. "We simply want to slow it down so we can handle it."

POPULATION SHIFTS AFFECT SCHOOLS [2]

Dozens of school districts throughout the suburban areas of New York City faced with shifts in student population unforeseen . . . [a few] years ago, are being confronted with prospects of either drastic shortages or surpluses of educational facilities.

In many cases, these changes will lead to the abandonment of expensive school buildings or construction of new ones.

The costs, even in one school district, can run to the tens of millions of dollars. Involved, too, is the increase in the busing of school children, with all the emotional ramifications, the redrawing of district lines and either the overcrowding or the underutilization of classrooms.

[2] From "Population Shifts Upsetting the Planning and Use of Suburban Schools Here," by David A. Andelman, staff correspondent. New York *Times*. p 75. Ap. 9, '73. © 1973 by The New York Times Company. Reprinted by permission.

In part, the problems are attributable to the trends in populations: shifts from the old suburbs that were booming in the 1950s and early 1960s to the new suburban areas opening up today; to faulty population projections, off by as much as 100 per cent over five-year periods, and to antiquated state laws barring interdistrict cooperation.

Building and Closing

As a consequence, for example, the Middle Island District in central Suffolk County is being forced to embark on a nearly $13 million building program for four new schools while the Commack School District, only twelve miles to the west, is talking of closing three schools—in both cases within the next six years.

"The error was made by many districts in the early fifties," said Nickolaus Engelhardt whose educational consulting firm of Engelhardt & Engelhardt in White Plains has been studying this problem since 1946. "School construction predictions were based on the high birthrate of the time. But it is very low at the moment. I don't think it will drop much below what it is now. Of course, that's a pure guess—everything is when you talk about birthrates."

He pointed to the situation of the Amity Regional School District outside New Haven, where the birthrate is down to seven per thousand—half the national average. "They just aren't having kids," Mr. Engelhardt said.

His conclusion is that if the new school districts based their population projection on this low birthrate, some of the errors of the past might be avoided. But the variables seem endless.

"There is no question that over the years in the 1950s the older suburban areas were growing rapidly," said William B. Haessig, director of educational facilities planning for the New York State Department of Education. "Now their population is trailing off and the new suburban areas are booming."

The result, Mr. Haessig concluded, is that "in some

cases it has provided a kind of instant urban renewal," in closing down old and unneeded excess schools, but in other areas, "by planning ahead for ten years, they have had newer buildings that are not even being used."

Benefits for Some

In some districts, the population shifts have been a boon, with older schools, overcrowded for twenty years and built originally on a shoestring budget with inadequate library space, no specialized music, art or trade rooms, now able to relax.

In East Meadow, Long Island, for instance, such general-purpose classrooms are now being converted to larger libraries, to rooms for the handicapped and for instruction in music, art and other specialties. But such serendipity is the exception rather than the rule.

School officials, planning experts and educators all seem to agree that misconceived school construction of the . . . [recent] years and the pitfalls of the next decade can be attributed to population projections.

"We find it difficult to project concrete population trends for more than five years, let alone ten," said Arthur Kunz, planning director for the Nassau-Suffolk Regional Planning Board.

Yet there are school districts that are already confidently predicting school enrollments for the year 1985. Middle Island, for instance, where nearly two thirds of its fifty-four square miles of territory is now vacant land with no immediate concrete plans for development, has nevertheless determined that its elementary school population will rise from the 2,370 pupils today to precisely 4,764 pupils in 1978.

The experience in such precise projections, however, has not been good. In 1965, the Westchester County Planning Department, showing a population of 853,000, projected a 90,000 increase by 1970. The department was wrong by more than 100 per cent. The actual increase was 40,000.

On Long Island, more than 50 per cent of the school districts in the older areas, particularly Nassau County, have shown sharp declines in school population in the last five years. The declines have also spilled over into the older, western areas of Suffolk County—the townships of Huntington, Babylon, Islip and the western portion of Smithtown. But farther east, the pattern has been dramatically reversed. The school districts in the Township of Brookhaven, the fastest growing in New York State, have shown equally marked increases in the last five years.

As a result, ten costly schools will be closed in western Suffolk County and six in eastern Nassau within the next . . . [few] years while four central Suffolk school districts, . . . [in March 1973] alone, went to the voters for approval of nearly $50 million in school construction bonds to build twelve new schools.

In the fast-growing suburbs of central and southern New Jersey, eighteen districts built new schools last year, according to Charles N. Updike, assistant director of the Bureau of Facility and Planning in the New Jersey Department of Education. A total of $175 million was spent on construction, although much of that money was spent on renovations and additions to existing schools.

Here too, however, the older New Jersey suburban areas have been closing facilities. Some old schools have been converted to administrative offices, school warehouses and maintenance centers; sometimes they are used by other municipal government agencies or demolished and the land sold.

Less Tangible Factors

All of these changes are expensive for the local taxpayer. School, business and financial experts estimate that a substantial new building program may add 7 to 10 per cent to the over-all school tax budget for the average taxpayer over the thirty-year life of a conventional bond issue.

In Middle Island, for instance, the $13 million building

program will add $2.75 to the current district tax rate of $23.78 per $100 of assessed valuation, or an increase of $123.75 a year for a home assessed at $4,500.

But there are other difficulties inherent in the problems of opening and closing of schools beyond the problem of cost and economics—less tangible factors that are frequently even more volatile. School district lines must be redrawn, children bused, teachers hired or laid off, a choice made for double or triple sessions.

Twenty-five years ago, when the area of Levittown, Long Island, the first major suburban development on Long Island, was experiencing its first growing pains in its school district, a decision was made not to undertake major building.

Hence, the Levittown schools have been on double sessions for twenty years, as have the schools of nearby Hicksville, which began growing at about the same time, according to state officials.

"They will begin tapering off one of these days," said Mr. Haessig of the State Education Department. "But that's a prospect that many of the new districts farther from the metropolitan area do not want to face."

Nevertheless, some may have to do so. Voters in the Sachem, Long Island, school district . . . [in March 1973] vetoed a $12 million building program for a junior high school and three elementary schools—the third time in fifteen months that the bond proposal was rejected. . . .

A resistance to integration and busing and the "sacred cow of the neighborhood school," as one educator expressed it, has . . . prevented in New York, but not in New Jersey, one solution to the problem of varying school populations: the regional school.

"There is a definite trend in New Jersey to regional schools," Mr. Updike of the State Education Department in Trenton said. "These are really a marriage of convenience because some school districts really do not have the student population to support their own schools."

Connecticut, too, has been experimenting with regional schools, particularly in the suburban areas of some of its larger cities, such as Hartford and New Haven.

According to the Connecticut Public Expenditure Council, a private public-interest group, Connecticut's elementary-school enrollment—where population trends are most quickly discernible—is projected to drop from . . . 471,000 . . . [in 1973] to 426,000 in the fall of 1977, or nearly 10 per cent over . . . four years.

The City of Norwalk, for instance, was planning a $15 million building program when the White Plains consulting concern of Raymond, Parish and Pine advised them that within a few years the schools could expect 3,500 empty seats. The high school, the consultants conceded, would be crowded for five to eight years, but in ten years there would be no crowding at all. So the building funds instead were used to fix up an abandoned high school and other schools in the district rather than to build new schools that would soon be half empty.

AGE AND CRIME [3]

A major increase in the number of young people in the age group most likely to commit crimes was an underlying reason for the rapid surge in the District of Columbia crime rates during the 1960s, according to a new analysis of crime and census data.

The analysis, made public . . . by the nonprofit Washington Center for Metropolitan Studies, also notes that the city gained elderly persons and single women, both likely to be crime victims, at the same time its population of fifteen- to twenty-four-year-olds grew.

"The crime rise does not mean that people are getting worse, but that there is a rise in the proportion of people who are in the most crime-prone age group (fifteen to

[3] From "D.C. Population Studied: Age Called a Factor in Crime," by Lawrence Feinberg, staff correspondent. Washington *Post.* p 1+. Je. 18, '73. © The Washington Post. Reprinted by permission.

twenty-four)," said Eunice Grier, a senior associate at the Center who wrote the new study.

"What causes crime is very complex," Mrs. Grier continued, "and we can't just look for relatively simple answers, like low income, race, or age, but age is a very important factor."

According to figures in the new study, the number of persons aged fifteen to twenty-four—the group that commits the most crime nationwide as well as in Washington—increased by 33 per cent in the city between 1960 and 1970, while Washington's overall population declined slightly.

In the same ten years the rate of serious crime in the District rose by about 350 per cent.

By contrast, the rate of serious crime in D.C. rose by only 11 per cent between 1950 and 1960—years in which the proportion of fifteen- to twenty-four-year-olds in the city population remained steady.

"After they [criminals] reach twenty-five they usually settle down or peter out," one D.C. police official commented. "They marry and get a stake in society, or they get so hooked on drugs that they don't function."

According to police statistics, about 70 per cent of the persons arrested in D.C. for serious crimes . . . [in 1972] were under age twenty-five—a proportion that has remained about the same for several decades.

Between 1950 and 1970 the number of persons over age sixty-five in Washington rose by 14,000—a 25 per cent increase while the total population fell by about 6 per cent.

The number of "singles" of various sorts also rose—an increase of 19,000 (37 per cent) in the number of individuals who are divorced or separated, and a 17 per cent rise in persons (over age fourteen) who have never been married.

Among the singles, women predominate, the Center report says.

In 1970 there were nearly 57,000 more single women than single men living in Washington, and at the time of the 1970 census, about 60 per cent of all women in the city (over age fourteen) were not currently married.

For the rest of the metropolitan area the proportion of single women was about what it is nationwide—40 per cent.

"Single women living alone are more likely to be subject to criminal attack and in need of police protection [and] this crime-vulnerable group has increased in numbers simultaneously with the youth group most likely to commit criminal attacks," the report notes.

Between 1950 and 1970, the number of blacks in Washington rose by 92 per cent, while the number of whites fell by 60 per cent.

However, the increase in the black population was much steeper between 1950 and 1960 . . . , when the crime rate was relatively stable, than it was between 1960 and 1970 . . . when the crime rate soared.

The increase in young blacks—age fifteen to twenty-four —was much greater, though, in the second decade—an 88 per cent rise between 1960 and 1970, compared to a 30 per cent increase between 1950 and 1960.

Overall, the report, like other census studies issued earlier, indicates that since 1950 Washington has lost large numbers of residents in their prime wage-earning and taxpaying years, while gaining more school children, elderly persons, and youths in their teens and early twenties—all groups that place heavy demands on public services.

Paradoxically, average income and educational levels in the city have risen during the past two decades, but so have the measures of social disorganization.

One of the most significant of these is the number of households headed by women with children under age eighteen. Between 1960 and 1970 this group rose from 14,000 to 24,000—an increase of 71 per cent. In all, about 14 per cent of D.C. households in 1970, were headed by women with young children.

According to the 1970 census, the average income of these female-headed families was only 60 per cent of the average for all families. Families headed by women also were three times more likely to be under the poverty line than were families headed by men.

The crimes counted by the police department in computing the rate for serious crime are: murder, rape, robbery, aggravated assault, burglary, larceny over $50 in value, and auto theft.

The number of these crimes per 100,000 population was 1,540 in 1950 in D.C. It rose slightly to 1,719 in 1960, and then soared to 7,814 in 1970.

Since then the crime rate has dropped, according to police, to 6,801 in 1971 and 4,969 in 1972.

Police officials generally attribute this to the larger size of the police force, better street lighting, and heroin control and treatment programs.

But Mrs. Grier said there may also have been a slowdown in the growth of the fifteen- to twenty-four-year-old age group, although exact figures will not be available until the next census in 1980.

RESULTS OF SLOWER GROWTH [4]

Reprinted from *U.S. News & World Report.*

A picture of a dramatically altered America within three decades is emerging from official reappraisal of US population changes.

These studies suggest that population growth, a trend as old as the country, may be on the threshold of leveling off far sooner than expected.

Latest indicator: A United States Census Bureau report issued on December 18 [1972] indicates that the nation's fertility rate in 1972 appears certain to hit a record low—just a shade over two births per woman.

At that rate, population increases would slow noticeably in years ahead until increases would almost stop altogether.

[4] From "Population Slowdown—What It Means to U.S." *U.S. News & World Report.* 73:59-62. D. 25, '72.

If this development proves permanent—and nobody can be sure of that yet—its effects on the country's future will be wide-reaching.

Among the likely consequences seen by population experts in and out of Government:

An older population—and perhaps one more conservative and resistant to change

A shift in public spending, with relatively less going for schools and more going for health care, pensions and combating social ills of the cities

Continued expansion of the US economy—but new challenges for businesses heavily involved in youth markets (Opportunities for firms dealing in services and luxury goods, however, could be expected to grow.)

Increasing financial problems for local governments in rural areas, where today's outward migration, if continued, would accelerate population declines

Unexpectedly early arrival of a "no-growth level" of fertility has caused the Census Bureau to issue new population projections—although not outright predictions—lower than any the agency ever considered before. . . .

[In 1971] the Census Bureau projected the nation's population range in the year 2000 from 271 million to 322 million persons. Under the new outlook, reflecting the drastic decline in fertility assumptions, estimates vary from a low of 251 million to a high of 300 million by the end of this century.

Authorities caution that one year's experience does not mean the United States will stop growing overnight. Population is expected to keep increasing for several decades, even with a continued low fertility rate, because of the large number of American women of childbearing age already living.

Meaning of Zero Growth

But the downward slide in births, along with lower birth expectations of young married women, is spurring demographers to examine what the advent of zero population growth would mean to this country.

Authorities emphasize that achieving a stable population would not mean all parts of the country would become static in number of residents.

Rural areas and small towns that count on a high rate of reproduction to offset outmigration are likely to lose residents quickly, authorities believe. Even suburban communities, which have grown fastest of all in recent years, might stop expanding.

Population trends in large central cities depend less on the national fertility rate than on each city's economic and social attractions, researchers conclude.

Fewer Schools, More Services

A stable population would mean mixed results for most communities, in the view of experts. They point out that steadily increasing demand for schools would level off or perhaps even decline as youngsters make up a smaller proportion of residents.

Demand for other public services, such as sewers and streets, might also shrink.

But some cities and towns could have trouble paying off long-term public debts already incurred if their populations and property-tax bases dwindle.

One possible result foreseen by authorities: mergers of local governments in order to share expenses.

Consultants expect that even as pressure for public schools diminished, college enrollment would increase. Parents of small families would be better able to afford college for their children, it is reckoned, and campuses also would be needed to retrain people thrown out of work by economic effects of shifts in the age mix.

Stabilization of the US population, experts warn, would not automatically solve all the nation's social and ecological problems.

They note that there are many causes other than overcrowding for crime, poverty, traffic jams, and other troubles that face the country.

"But population levels do affect our ability to cope with social, economic and environmental problems and our ability to pay the costs," asserts one Government economist. He added: "With a stabilized population, more of the increases in our gross national product can be used to escape the consequences of congestion and growing numbers."

One thing on which most experts agree: An end to population growth would mean more women seeking careers outside the home.

It's true, economists say, that some women now work only to help support their families, and there would be less need for that with fewer children. But labor consultants predict that, in a no-growth era, more women would devote themselves to full-time jobs in fields where they intend to spend all their working lives. The number of married couples with no children may rise, observers say.

Many businesses would have to adjust in order to survive in a country where population growth is slowing down. Some firms oriented to the infant and youth markets, for instance, might have to shift emphasis to adult or perhaps more precisely to elderly customers.

Many economists contend that as the US population levels off, per capita income will rise. Sharp increases are foreseen in spending for nonessentials such as travel, second homes, recreation, entertainment and gourmet foods.

A sustained low level of births also would drastically alter the US demographic profile—mainly by raising the average age of Americans and leaving the country with more older people than young. . . .

More Older People

Many demographers, such as Norman Ryder, of Princeton University, say that uneven distribution of age groups is as important as the country's total members.

Mr. Ryder says the US population already "is grossly

maldistributed by age, with few people around age thirty-five, many around age fifteen and few around age five." He asserts: "We pay dearly for these variations, because many sectors of society deal with particular age groups—the schools, the labor market, the Social Security system—and are strained by the need to contract or expand."

Some scientists worry that a society top-heavy with older people might limit chances for the young to advance to positions of responsibility and authority.

Others voice concern that if the average age of Americans climbs markedly, the United States might reject its heritage of innovation and turn resistant to change and experiment.

Opponents of this theory argue that this has not happened to countries such as Sweden, a nation where the population has remained stable but which still is considered a leader in many new social programs.

This, too, is foreseen by economists: With older and more experienced workers, the United States would see a rise in labor efficiency and industrial productivity. Others, however, warn that fewer young workers entering the labor force could restrict the source of many fresh ideas.

Retirement Effects

Government officials and businessmen are certain to take a close look at new lower population projections with an eye to their effect on retirement programs.

One possibility is that if the number of people living on pensions grows significantly in relation to active workers who finance retirement plans, benefits might have to be reduced or contributions increased.

Although the sharp drop in births and fertility rate in 1972 caught most authorities by surprise . . . , a general trend toward smaller families has prevailed in the United States almost without interruption for fifteen years.

The average fertility rate of [2.025] children per woman

. . . [is] less than the record US low set in 1936 during the depression.

A fertility rate of [2.025 is] slightly under the target of 2.1 set by proponents of zero population growth. Retaining an average of 2.1 children per woman, experts figure, eventually would halt population expansion except for that caused by immigration.

Many reasons are cited for the trend to smaller families: Increased use of contraceptives, liberalized abortion laws, the "women's liberation" movement, later marriages, economic considerations and concern for the environment.

With a steady fertility rate of 1.8 children per woman, authorities predict the nation would virtually stop growing in about fifty years—instead of the seventy to eighty years forecast under higher rates—and thereafter go into a decline.

Population experts note that US birthrates have surged up and down before, and they are cautious about making any firm predictions on the basis of the startlingly low figures for 1972.

"Safest Prediction"

The Census Bureau itself points out that it had little success in forecasting the country's growth over just the two-year period from 1970 to 1972. Actual births turned out to be about 5 per cent under the Bureau's lowest figure —an overestimate of some 400,000.

Says one demographer: "One of the safest predictions about long-range projections is that they will be incorrect in some significant aspect."

Proponents of reduced population growth express guarded jubilation at Census Bureau reports of fewer births and lower fertility expectations.

Said a spokesman for the Population Reference Bureau, Inc., a private and nonprofit organization based in Washington, D. C.:

The current decline in fertility, which started in 1958, has given rise to predictions that population growth in the United

States will soon stop. The same kind of predictions were made back in the 1930s, and they didn't come true then. It's unlikely that they will come true in the 1970s, either.

The group's official added, however, that they do not expect a repetition of the "baby boom" that hit the United States after World War II.

Paul Ehrlich, Stanford University biologist who has been a leader in the zero-population-growth movement, called the birth slowdown "cheering." But he urged that the fertility rate be dropped even under the replacement level of 2.1 children per woman.

Dr. Ehrlich explained:

It is very important to realize that if we stay at this level, the population size will hit the vicinity of 300 million or more before growth stops. In my estimation, that would mean at least a doubling of our environmental and resource problems regardless of what technological remedies one could employ.

POPULATION AND BUSINESS [5]

A decade ago Gerber Products sold as high as 32 times earnings, and even . . . [in 1971] was at 22 times earnings. It was a growth stock. . . . [In 1972] in a rising market it [sold] for barely 14 times probable 1972 earnings. It [had] fallen from grace.

Why? . . . Gerber has chiefly to do with babies, and things to do with babies no longer titillate The Street. The Baby Boom has turned into a Baby Bust.

It all happened so suddenly. The alarmists were still crying about the population explosion when it was already turning into an echo. In the early sixties, there were around 116 births per year for every one thousand American women of childbearing age. At that time, in her lifetime, the aver-

[5] From "If You're a Businessman, This Chart May Be the Shape of Your Future." *Forbes.* 110:37-44. S. 1, '72. Reprinted by permission of *Forbes* magazine.

age woman would have 3.6 children, enough to replace her and her husband and enough left over to put a big bang into the population explosion. By the first four months of 1972, the birthrate had dropped to the point where the average woman would have only 2.1 children in her child-bearing span. At the new figure, she and her husband would not quite be reproducing themselves, for a certain number of children will die before maturity or will never marry.

No, zero population growth isn't here yet. It won't be for a long time. The United States is still a young nation, and while the birthrate is low, so is the death rate. But as the proportion of children declines and today's young become tomorrow's old, the death rate will rise. It will take roughly seventy years at current rates for the two lines to cross and for the population to level off. In the meantime, the important thing is this: The rate of population growth will get smaller and smaller.

There are those who think the birthrate will rise again, but the trend of history is against them. Ironing out temporary squiggles like that after World War II, the US birthrate has trended down since around 1800.

Changing Attitude

Along with changes in life styles, there have been changes in attitudes towards family size. In 1967 a Gallup Poll showed 40 percent wanted four or more children and in 1971 this figure dropped to 23 percent. Another survey revealed that 80 percent felt there was nothing wrong with childless marriages.

What are the business and political implications? Are they worrisome? Alfred Sauvy, the distinguished French demographer, thinks so. In his book *General Theory of Population,* he argues that France's social, cultural and economic ills are the direct result of the fact that its population has remained virtually stable for more than a century. A growing population is a stimulus to society, he says; a nation with a stagnant population eventually will stagnate.

On the other hand, look at Japan. "The Japanese miracle" in part is a result of the government's drive to cut the birthrate sharply by encouraging abortions. Had it not done so, the result might have been catastrophic. Already suffocatingly crowded, Japan might have become unlivable.

After studying the problem, the President's Commission on Population Growth and the American Future concluded:

> We have looked for, and have not found, any convincing economic argument for continuing national population growth. The health of the economy does not depend on it. The vitality of business does not depend on it. The welfare of the average person certainly does not depend on it.
>
> In fact, the average person will be markedly better off in terms of traditional economic values if population growth follows the two-child projection rather than the three-child one. Slower growth will give us an older population and this trend will require adjustments. . . . [However, these adjustments are] well within the ability of the nation to provide.

Perhaps that last sentence is the key; perhaps whether a nation profits from slow population growth or gets into trouble depends on whether the people can make the necessary adjustments. In this connection, one has to consider the differences in the French and the Japanese characters. The French are a highly individualistic people, almost an anarchistic one; they are constantly in conflict with each other and have been for hundreds of years. In contrast, the Japanese are a well-disciplined people with an extremely strong social sense. In Japan, capital, labor, the banks and the government all work together as one.

What about the American character? One can only speculate about it. In explaining the sharp decline in the birthrate, some experts point out that women coming of childbearing age today were born in "the era of Spock." They were reared "permissively." Their parents indulged their every wish and they grew up not with the Puritan ethic but as hedonists. They don't want the expense and trouble of bringing up a large family if that means sacrificing anything for themselves, whether a swimming pool or a holiday in Europe.

On the Other Hand

A people who have rejected the Puritan ethic for hedonism don't seem like the stuff on which a nation can thrive economically. However, other experts point out that another reason for the decline in the birthrate is that more and more women are entering the labor force, staying longer and marrying later. It's a truism among demographers that "the later the less." In addition, more and more women are career-minded; they go back into the labor force as soon as their children are ready for school. That hardly makes them seem like hedonists. Or does it?

All that is a matter for speculation. Meanwhile, this much is certain: A nation in which the average family has two children will have a higher per capita income than one in which the average family has three. It's a matter of simple arithmetic: If the family has an income of $10,000 a year, three children will mean a per capita income of $2,000; two children, $2,500.

This means that in the years to come an increasing number of Americans will have more *disposable* income, for travel, for entertainment, for a house at the beach, for a motorboat. People won't eat more, but they will eat more convenience foods, more gourmet foods, on which the profit margins are higher.

In a study entitled *The Demography of the 1970s: The Birth Dearth and What It Means,* Ben J. Wattenberg, a leading writer on population trends, cites figures to show that in 1985 Americans will be spending 79 percent more on food, drink and tobacco than in 1968 in terms of 1968 dollars; 95 percent more on clothing and clothing materials; 107 percent more on transportation; 110 percent more on household operation and furnishings; 149 percent more on recreation, education and the like; 172 percent more on housing; 185 percent more on personal and medical care.

Meanwhile, certain developments already are taking place: The work force is growing larger, both in numbers and in percentage of the population. This is one reason (though not the only reason) for the persistence of unemployment despite the upturn in business. The problem will get increasingly acute. The economy will have to run faster and faster just to stand still.

At any rate, the economic consequences are already visible. According to Susanne Stoiber, assistant to the executive director of the Committee for National Health Insurance, the nation's maternity wards are running at only 40 percent of capacity, even though other hospital wards are overcrowded. This obviously is a terrible waste of money and space. The committee's solution: for the hospitals in each community or region to get together and work out a rational plan, under which some will take on the maternity load of the others, while the others use the wards thus emptied to relieve the overcrowding.

What Classroom Shortage?

There has been a sharp drop also in the school population. Only a few years ago, as recently as the middle sixties, there was a severe shortage of classrooms in the United States and a severe shortage of teachers. Every suburb was under pressure to build more schools and hire more teachers. In almost every suburb, the most bitterly fought political issue was whether to raise school taxes, whether to float another series of bonds to build another school. Except in a few communities, this issue has disappeared.

The school population, says Dr. Sidney P. Marland Jr., [former] United States Commissioner of Education [now Assistant Secretary for Education],

peaked somewhere in 1970 at 51.4 million, and in the ensuing two years we have begun to drop in total elementary and secondary education to a number now about 50.4 million, or down about one million children from the peak of 1970. Most of the reduction occurred in the elementary schools. At the moment, the secondary schools—we'll call them for the purposes of statistics grades nine through twelve—are stable. Somewhere between 1972 and 1975 we'll begin to see a decline in the secondary schools, reflecting the present decline in elementary schools. By 1980 we'll be down a million and a half.

In the sixties there was a shortage of teachers; salaries, obeying the law of supply and demand, soared. At the same time, students poured into the schools of education. This was partly because teachers' salaries had become attractive and partly because the shortage caused many draft boards to exempt teachers. Now there is a teacher glut. The National Education Association estimates that more than 130,000 of the nation's over 3 million teachers are unemployed. "This will be a continuing situation," Dr. Marland says. "Thousands of teachers in the United States will just have to go into other professions."

Thousands have already been forced into driving cabs, waiting on tables, working behind store counters, becoming an intellectual proletariat, with what social and political consequences one can only guess at.

The drop in the birthrate has already created what Dr. Michael Sumichrast, chief economist of the National Association of Homebuilders, calls a revolution in homebuilding —a switch from detached houses to condominiums. Dr. Sumichrast says:

> It started overnight—two years ago, a year and a half ago. Take Washington. A year and a half ago there was just one project in Washington. Today there are nearly fifty. It's that kind of fantastic change. And it's happening not only in Washington, but in just about every other city.
>
> These are people who have no kids. My wife is doing a study of one project. I looked at it. In this project, about 70 percent have no children. And only 5 percent have more than three.

According to Dr. Sumichrast, the average condominium apartment has roughly half the floor space of the average house. In Washington, he says, "a typical house has 2,500 square feet. These condominium apartments start from 900 and go to 1,200."

Naturally, he says, they sell for about half the price. This gives the condominium owners more expendable income for things like travel, boating, skiing. And second homes. "It's amazing, the growth of the second-home market," Dr. Sumichrast says.

The growth of the condominiums also is bound to have an effect on the home furnishings industry and the household-equipment industry: smaller and fewer units, but probably of better and better quality and higher price. For example, Dr. Sumichrast says that couples who buy apartments in condominiums usually insist on a king-size bedroom because they want to furnish it with a king-size bed.

Repairless Equipment?

One company that appears to have done more than thought about the implications of the declining birthrate is Whirlpool Corporation, which hired a group of five prominent university professors to study it. John Smallwood, director of economic & marketing research of Whirlpool, was in charge. He says people are bound to demand smaller appliances, appliances "capable of storage somewhere where they will still be visible but blend into the surroundings better, appliances which do a number of things in order to save space." He also believes it will be necessary for companies like his to make appliances that never need repairs. A wife with a job can't sit around the house all day waiting for a repairman, he points out.

Another company that has given a good deal of thought to the decline in the birthrate is, understandably enough, Gerber Products, the nation's leading manufacturer of baby foods. Says William Francis, sales forecasting supervisor:

We've gone into a line of nonfoods—clothing, knitwear pants and shirts and socks for children, distributed through grocery outlets, a line of sleepwear for children, distributed through department stores. If we can keep mothers our customers for another six months, it's like another two million births. We have a certain amount of sales at the old end of the market right now; for many years now, old people have been using our baby foods for their soft diets. That market should grow.

As smart a marketing company as Johnson & Johnson has started to roll with the punches. It is now running television commercials that show hard-hatted workers using Johnson's Baby Powder.

Says Dr. Patrick Lynch, director of corporate development at Westinghouse Electric Corporation:

The most immediate concern to us is the changing life style, the changing social values, which are really at the heart, we think, of the change in population growth. Population growth changes are really symptomatic of something much deeper, and it is those things we must be concerned about in running our business —the changing attitudes toward life, how people want to run their lives, their concern with the environment and with the good life; these are having a much more immediate effect on us than the change in numbers. Two thirds of what we do is involved in power systems. The concern with the environment has encouraged the development of nuclear power.

Dr. Lynch believes that as the population grows older, "what we are going to see are subsidies by the Government to increase health-care delivery, to try to upgrade preventive health care, and these are areas in which we think we can provide some service."

At Melville Shoe, President Francis Rooney, Jr., is sure the drop in the birthrate will lead shoe buyers to "upgrade." He says:

I think the trend of women working and, therefore, adding to the family income, plus the new life style—not just staying at home barefoot and pregnant—makes women more viable customers. They won't have a guilt complex about spending the income of their husbands to buy a new dress or shoes.

Dr. Seymour Marshak, manager of market research at Ford, says of the decline in the birthrate and the consequent rise in per capita income: "It could mean that cars will become more luxurious, since people will have more in the way of discretionary funds. More luxurious but smaller."

Borden Inc.'s vice president in charge of marketing, Clayton Rohrback, anticipates a change in the mix of Bor-

den's sales and in the packaging. In addition, he believes
that small, smart food companies may prove able to react
more swiftly to the changes in life style that appear to have
brought about the drop in the birthrate than some larger
companies. He says:

> In a large company, you have products that sell through all
> age groups, with specific emphasis of some products on specific
> ages. For example, Cracker Jack is eaten mainly by small chil-
> dren; so, if there are fewer of them, the task for Cracker Jack is
> to get more people to eat it, by means of conventional marketing
> methods. While smaller kids are decreasing in number, the thir-
> teen- to eighteen-year-olds are growing in number, and they hap-
> pen to be a big potato-chip group, so what we may be losing on
> Cracker Jack we may be picking up on potato chips. In the long
> run, I think you will see more and more foods that are packaged
> for the smaller family—like frozen peas packaged for two. We're
> already getting letters from people saying why don't we put out
> something or other in a small package. We've already done that
> with our instant potatoes.

How GE Sees It

General Electric's chief economist, Dr. R. S. Villanueva,
makes economic forecasts four times a year and a long-range
forecast every three years. Like many other economists, he
considers the decline in the birthrate inseparable from the
change in living style. The services he sees as the businesses
of the future are entertainment, learning, medical facilities
and mass transportation.

Not every US corporation has considered what the decline in the birthrate will mean to its business. Several of
those queried by *Forbes* insisted that it probably was just
temporary; there would be another upsurge soon, they said,
just like the upsurge in the fifties. Others shrugged their
shoulders and said there was nothing they could do. A
spokesman at Colgate-Palmolive said, "We're in consumer
goods," and conceded, "the thought is there, but nothing in
general has been done; probably we should be doing something."

That's one way of looking at things, but it's a shortsighted way. The change has already dropped Gerber from the growth-stock category to the lowly cyclical. It may well do the same with other companies. There are companies now selling at ten times earnings that will be growth stocks because of the empty hospital cribs. The change in the birthrate will cause some companies to fade and others to flourish. It is probably the most momentous thing that has happened to US business in a couple of decades.

BIBLIOGRAPHY

An asterisk (*) preceding a reference indicates that the article or part of it has been reprinted in this book.

BOOKS, PAMPHLETS, AND DOCUMENTS

Allen, D. L. Population, resources and the great complexity. (PRB Selection no 29) Population Reference Bureau. 1755 Massachusetts Ave. N.W. Washington, D.C. 20036. '69.

Bachrach, Peter and Bergman, Elihu. Choice and power: the formation of American population policy. Lexington Books. '73.

Berelson, Bernard. Beyond family planning. (Studies in family planning, no 38) Population Council. 245 Park Ave. New York 10017. '69.

Buckley, Mary. The aged are people too: about William Posner and social work with the old. Kennikat Press. '72.

Burgess, E. W. ed. Aging in western societies. University of Chicago Press. '60.

Callahan, D. J. Abortion: law, choice, and morality. Macmillan. '70.

Callahan, D. J. ed. The American population debate. Doubleday. '71.

Chamberlain, N. W. Beyond Malthus; population and power. Basic Books. '70.

Clark, Margaret and Anderson, B. G. Culture and aging: an anthropological study of older Americans. C. C. Thomas. '67.

Commoner, Barry. The closing circle: nature, man and technology. Knopf. '71.

Curtin, S. R. Nobody ever died of old age. Little. '72.

Ehrlich, A. H. and Ehrlich, P. R. Population, resources, environment: issues in human ecology. Freeman. '72.

Ehrlich, P. R. The population bomb. Ballantine. '71.

Ehrlich, P. R. and others. Human ecology: problems and solutions. Freeman. '73.

Etzioni, Amitai. Genetic fix: new opportunities for you, your child and the nation. Macmillan. '73.

Ewald, W. R. Jr. ed. Environment and change: the next fifty years. Indiana University Press. '68.

Fisher, Tadd. Our overcrowded world. Parents' Magazine Press. '69.

175

Fraser, Dean. The people problem: what you should know about growing population & vanishing resources. Indiana University Press. '73.

Frejka, Tomaš. The future of population growth; alternative paths to equilibrium. Wiley. '73.

Group for the Advancement of Psychiatry. Committee on Preventive Psychiatry. Humane reproduction. Scribner's. '74.

Hauser, P. M. ed. The population dilemma. Prentice-Hall. '71.

Hauser, P. M. and Duncan, O. D. eds. The study of population: an inventory and appraisal. University of Chicago Press. '59.

Heer, D. M. comp. Readings on population. Prentice-Hall. '68.

Heer, D. M. Society and population. Prentice-Hall. '68.

Hinrichs, Noël, ed. [for the Council on Population and Environment] Population, environment and people. McGraw. '72.

Hodge, P. L. and Hauser, P. M. Challenge of America's metropolitan population outlook; 1960 to 1985. Praeger. '68.

Horsley, Kathryn and others. Options: a study guide to population and the American future. Population Reference Bureau. 1755 Massachusetts Ave. N.W. Washington, D.C. 20036. '73.

Hughes, H. M. ed. Population growth and the complex society. Allyn. '72.

Kammeyer, K. C. W. An introduction to population. Chandler. '71.

Kammeyer, K. C. W. ed. Population studies; selected essays and research. Rand McNally. '69.

Landsberg, H. H. and others. Natural resources for U.S. growth; a look ahead to the year 2000. Resources for the Future, Inc. 1755 Massachusetts Ave. N.W. Washington, D.C. 20036. '64.

Landsberg, H. H. and others. Resources in America's future; patterns of requirements and availabilities, 1960-2000. Resources for the Future, Inc. 1755 Massachusetts Ave. N.W. Washington, D.C. 20036. '63.

*League of Women Voters of the United States. More? The interfaces between population, economic growth and the environment. The League. 1730 M St. N.W. Washington, D.C. 20036. '72.

Malthus, Thomas. An essay on population. Dutton. '58.

Meadows, D. H. and others. The limits to growth: a report for the Club of Rome's project on the predicament of mankind. Universe. '72.

Meadows, Dennis and others. Dynamics of growth in a finite world. Wright-Allen. '73.

Miles, R. E. Jr. Man's population predicament. (Population Bul. v 27 no 2) Population Reference Bureau. 1755 Massachusetts Ave. N.W. Washington, D.C. 20036. '70.

Miller, H. P. Population, pollution and affluence [based on address]. (PRB Selection no 36) Population Reference Bureau. 1755 Massachusetts Ave. N.W. Washington, D.C. 20036. '71.

Nam, C. B. ed. Population and society. Houghton. '68.

National Academy of Sciences. Office of the Foreign Secretary. Rapid population growth: consequences and policy implications. Johns Hopkins Press. '71.

National Committee on Urban Growth Policy. The new city; ed. by Donald Canty. Praeger. '69.

*Nixon, R. M. Established population growth commission; message from the President of the United States relative to population growth. (House Document no 91-139) 91st Congress; 1st session. U.S. Gov. Ptg. Office. Washington, D.C. 20401. '69.

Noonan, J. T. Jr. ed. The morality of abortion: legal and historical perspectives. Harvard University Press. '70.

Norton, E. H. Population growth and the future of black folk. Population Reference Bureau. 1755 Massachusetts Ave. N.W. Washington, D.C. 20036. '73.

Ogburn, Charlton, Jr. Population and resources: the coming collision. (Population Bul. v 26 no 2) Population Reference Bureau. 1755 Massachusetts Ave. N.W. Washington, D.C. 20036. '70.

Oppenheimer, V. K. Population. (Headline Series no 206) Foreign Policy Association. 345 E. 46th St. New York 10017. '71.

Petersen, William. Population. Macmillan. '69.

Pickard, J. P. Dimension of metropolitanism. (Research Monograph 14) Urban Land Institute. 1200 18th St. N.W. Washington, D.C. 20036. '67.

*Planned Parenthood Federation of America. Population policy: statement adopted by membership, 1972. The Federation. 810 Seventh Ave. New York 10019. '72.

*Planned Parenthood Federation of America. Teenage sexuality and family planning services to minors, [statement] adopted by the membership, October 26, 1972. The Federation. 810 Seventh Ave. New York 10019. '72.

Population Crisis Committee. Population problems and policies in economically advanced countries; report of a conference at Ditchley Park, England, Sept. 29-Oct. 2, 1972. The Committee. 1835 K St. N.W. Washington, D.C. 20006. '73.

Population Reference Bureau. Abortion: the continuing controversy. (Population Bul. v 28 no 4) The Bureau. 1755 Massachusetts Ave. N.W. Washington, D.C. 20036. '72.

Population Reference Bureau. People! an introduction to the
    study of population; ed. by R. C. Cook and Jane Lecht. Co-
    lumbia Books. '72.
Population Reference Bureau. Population activities of the United
    States government. (Population Bul. v 27, no 4) The Bureau.
    1755 Massachusetts Ave. N.W. Washington, D.C. 20036. '71.
Population Reference Bureau. Population statistics: what do they
    mean? The Bureau. 1755 Massachusetts Ave. N.W. Washing-
    ton, D.C. 20036. '72.
Population Reference Bureau. Population: the future is now;
    summary of the Population Commission's findings. (Popula-
    tion Bul. v 28 no 2) The Bureau. 1755 Massachusetts Ave.
    N.W. Washington, D.C. 20036. '72.
Population Reference Bureau. Techno-population race: who
    needs it? The Bureau. 1755 Massachusetts Ave. N.W. Wash-
    ington, D.C. 20036. '72.
Population Reference Bureau. Where will the next 50 million
    Americans live? (Population Bul. v 27, no 5) The Bureau.
    1755 Massachusetts Ave. N.W. Washington, D.C. 20036. '71.
Riley, M. W. and others. Aging and society. Russell Sage. '69. 3v.
Schaefer, L. M. An introduction to population, environment, and
    society. Spaulding Copy Center. Hamden, Conn. '72.
Singer, S. F. ed. Is there an optimum level of population? Mc-
    Graw-Hill. '71.
Smith, B. K. Aging in America. Beacon Press. '73.
Sorvall, Vivian. Overpopulation: how many are too many? Pen-
    dulum Press. '71.
Spengler, Joseph. Population change, modernization, and welfare.
    Prentice-Hall. '74.
Study of Critical Environmental Problems. Man's impact on the
    global environment; assessment and recommendations for
    action. M.I.T. Press. '70.
United States. Advisory Commission on Intergovernmental Rela-
    tions. Urban and rural America: policies for future growth;
    a Commission report. Supt. of Docs. Washington, D.C. 20402.
    '68.
United States. Commission on Population Growth and the Amer-
    ican Future. Economic aspects of population change; ed. by
    E. R. Morss and R. H. Reed. Supt. of Docs. Washington,
    D.C. 20402. '72.
*United States. Commission on Population Growth and the Amer-
    ican Future. Population growth and the American future; re-
    port. Supt. of Docs. Washington, D.C. 20402. '72.

Reprinted in this book: Dissenting opinion by John N. Erlenborn
p 156-7; Contraception for teenagers. p 109.

United States. Commission on Population Growth and the American Future. Population, resources, and the environment; ed. by R. G. Ridker. Supt. of Docs. Washington, D.C. 20402. '72.

United States. Congress. House of Representatives. Committee on Banking and Currency. Ad Hoc Subcommittee on Urban Growth. Population trends, hearings, June 3-July 31, 1969. 91st Congress, 1st session. Supt. of Docs. Washington, D.C. 20402. '69.

United States. Department of Agriculture. 1971 yearbook: a good life for more people. Supt. of Docs. Washington, D.C. 20402. '71.

*United States. Department of Commerce. Bureau of the Census. Birth expectations of American wives, June 1973. (Current Population Reports: Population Characteristics. Series P-20 no 254) Supt. of Docs. Washington, D.C. 20402. '73.

United States. Department of Commerce. Bureau of the Census. Estimates of population of the United States and components of change: 1940-1971. (Current Population Reports: Population Estimates and Projections. Series P-25 no 465) Supt. of Docs. Washington, D.C. 20402. '71.

United States. Department of Commerce. Bureau of the Census. Projections of the population of the United States by age and sex: 1970-2020. (Current Population Reports: Population Estimates and Projections. Series P-25 no 470) Supt. of Docs. Washington, D.C. 20402. '71.

United States. Department of Commerce. Bureau of the Census. We, the Americans. Supt. of Docs. Washington, D.C. 20402. '72-'73.
    A series of illustrated reports on the 1970 census. Booklets available: We, the Americans: who we are; We, the black Americans; We, the Americans: our homes; We, the American women.

United States. Executive Office of the President. Domestic Council Committee on National Growth. Report on national growth, 1972-   . Supt. of Docs. Washington, D.C. 20402. '72.

United States. National Goals Research Staff. Toward balanced growth: quantity with quality; report. Supt. of Docs. Washington, D.C. 20402. '70.

United States. President's Task Force on Rural Development. A new life for the country; report. Supt. of Docs. Washington, D.C. 20402. '70.

*United States Catholic Conference. Division of Family Life. Respect life. The Conference. 1312 Massachusetts Ave. N.W. Washington, D.C. 20005. '73.

Westoff, L. A. and Westoff, C. F. From now to zero; fertility, contraception and abortion in America. Little. '71.

*Zero Population Growth, Inc. A statement of the goals of Zero
   Population Growth, Inc. The organization. 1346 Connecticut
   Ave. N.W. Washington, D.C. 20036. n.d.

PERIODICALS

Aging. 205:10-11. N. '71. Pre-White House conference activities
   evoke many gains for the elderly.
America. 124:110. F. 6, '71. How many of us are there? P. S. Tem-
   plin.
America. 124:315-18. Mr. 27, '71. Growing old, and how to cope
   with it. Alfons Deeken.
America. 124:538-40. My. 22, '71. Zero population growth, do we
   need it now? T. C. Jermann.
America. 125:368-9+. N. 6, '71. Population growth and public pol-
   icy. J. T. McHugh.
America. 125:502. D. 11, '71. Growing minority.
America. 127:88-90. Ag. 19, '72. ZPG: a bourgeois conspiracy?
   J. H. Fichter.
America. 127:107. S. 2, '72. ZPG won't banish all problems.
America. 127:472-3. D. 2, '72. Senior power. Patrick Butler.
America. 128:81. F. 3, '73. Supreme Court on abortion.
America. 128:inside front cover. F. 10, '73. Of many things: con-
   stitutional right and abortion legislation. C. M. Whelan.
American Economic Review Papers & Proceedings. 61:392-8. My.
   '71. Impact of population on resources and the environment.
   J. L. Fisher.
American Economic Review Papers & Proceedings. 61:408-17. My.
   '71. Issues in the economics of a population policy for the
   United States. G. G. Cain.
Atlantic. 230:68-78. Jl. '72. Aging in the land of the young. Sharon
   Curtin.
Bulletin of the Atomic Scientists. 26:15-19. N. '70. Licensing: for
   cars and babies. B. M. Russett.
      Discussion. Bulletin of the Atomic Scientists. 27:2-3. My. '71.
Bulletin of the Atomic Scientists. 29:3. D. '73. Unlimited growth:
   a good? [letter]. Rudolph von Abele.
*Bulletin of the Council for Basic Education. 13:8-9. Ja. '69. Fur-
   ther doubts about sex education.
Business Week, p 66-8. Je. 3, '72. Surprising decline in the birth-
   rate.
Business Week. p 41-2. D. 15, '73. Burgeoning benefits of a lower
   birth rate.
Changing Times. 25:13-14. Ag. '71. America's new look, as the
   census sees it.
Christian Century. 88:1374. N. 24, '71. Birth dearth?

Christian Century. 89:780-1. Jl. 19, '72. National consultation on ethics and population policies. R. Dickinson.

Christian Century. 89:892-5. S. 13, '72. Pregnancy and the judgmental society. R. C. Wahlberg.

Christian Century. 90:195-7. F. 14, '73. Abortion decision: a balancing of rights. J. C. Evans.

Christian Century. 90:254-5. F. 28, '73. Confusion at the highest level. J. R. Nelson.

Christianity Today. 17:32-3. F. 16, '73. Abortion and the court.

Christianity Today. 17:48. F. 16, '73. Abortion decision: a death blow?

*Civil Liberties. No. 298:1-2. S. '73. New threats: saving abortion. Arlie Schardt.

Commentary. 53:45-52. My. '72. Population controllers. Samuel McCracken.

    Discussion. Commentary. 53:6+. My.; 54:10+, 30+. S. '72.

Commentary. 53:37-44. Je. '72. Growth and its enemies. Rudolf Klein.

    Discussion. Commentary. 54:24+. O. '72.

Commonweal. 96:418. Ag. 11, '72. Ehrlich vs. Commoner. John Deedy.

Commonweal. 97:435-6. F. 16, '73. Abortion decision.

    Discussion. Commonweal. 98:133-5. Ap. 13, '73.

Commonweal. 97:438-40. F. 16, '73. Abortion decision. R. F. Drinan.

    Reply with rejoinder. Conmonweal. 98:75+. Mr. 30, '73. J. T. McHugh.

Current. 132:42-5. S. '71. International action for the aged? A. L. Danzig.

*Daedalus. 102:15-29. Fall '73. Zero population growth: the goal and the means. Kingsley Davis.

*Daedalus. 102:35-8. Fall '73. Population and the American predicament: the case against complacency. J. P. Holdren.

Department of State Bulletin. 65:172-8. Ag. 16, '71. Population growth and national development; address, June 14, 1971. D. L. Gamon.

Dun's. 98:55. D. '71. Is there life after forty? Susan Margetts.

Econometrica. 40:109-36. Ja. '72. Population and optimum growth. John Pitchford.

Editorial Research Reports. v 2, no 20:905-24. N. 24, '71. Zero population growth. H. B. Shaffer.

*Evaluation. v 1, no 2:84-5. Summer '73. Zero population growth: do we really want it? Amitai Etzioni.

*Family Planning Perspectives. 2:9-11. O. '70. Unwanted births and U.S. population growth. Larry Bumpass and C. F. Westoff.

*Family Planning Perspectives. 4:10-15+. Ap. '72. Population and the American future: the Commission's final report. Richard Lincoln.

Field & Stream. 76:20+. Je. '71. We must stop population growth. W. H. Davis.

*Forbes. 110:37-44. S. 1, '72. If you're a businessman, this chart may be the shape of your future.

Fortune. 83:80-5+. F. '71. New questions about the U.S. population. L. A. Mayer.

Harper's Bazaar. 105:104-5. Ag. '72. No more willing baby machines. Isaac Asimov.

Intellect. 102:6. O. '73. Population proliferation and pollution; remarks. Sir Kingsley Dunham.

International Organization. 26:175-212. Spring '72. Population, resources, and technology: political implications of the environmental crisis. Nazli Choucri and J. P. Bennett.

Journal of Marriage and the Family. 35:89-92. F. '73. Population growth and family planning. Louise Corman and J. B. Schaefer.

Life. 72:46-50+. My. 19, '72. Crucial math of motherhood; recommendations of the presidential Commission on Population Growth.

Life. 73:52-3. D. 29, '72. Bottom drops out of the baby boom.

Mental Hygiene. 55:51-4. Ja. '71. Social values and the elderly. R. A. Kalish.

Monthly Labor Review. 94:14-21. N. '71. Economic growth and ecology—an economist's view. W. W. Heller.

Nation. 216:71-2. Ja. 15, '73. Population: problem for the populace. Hugh Downs.

Nation. 216:165. F. 5, '73. Jane Roe and Mary Doe: abortion ruling.

*Nation. 216:626-8. My. 14, '73. Senior power: aging in America. Barbara Isenberg.

National Review. 24:250-1. My. 12, '72. Conservative reacts: elements of a population policy. William Petersen.

National Review. 25:193. F. 16, '73. Death of pluralism? Right to abortion.

National Review. 25:249-50. Mr. 2, '73. Abortion front: end of the phony war.

National Review. 25:260-4. Mr. 2, '73. Raw judicial power. J. T. Noonan, Jr.

Nation's Business. 59:52-5. D. '71. Bye-bye, baby boom. Tom Kelly.

New Republic. 162:18-23. Ap. 4; 46-7. My. 9, '70. The nonsense explosion. B. J. Wattenberg.

New Republic. 164:15-17. F. 27, '71. Biological tyranny: OEO's family planning projects in West Virginia. W. M. Hern.

New Republic. 168:9. F. 10, '73. Abortion.
  Reply. New Republic. 168:32. Mr. 24, '73. M. P. O'Boyle.

New Republic. 170:10-11. Mr. 23, '74. Old people power. Fred Harris.

*New York Times. Sec 12. Ap. 30, '72. Population: the U. S. problem; the world crisis. [For copies write Population Supplement, P.O. Box 6586, Washington, D.C. 20009.
  Reprinted in this book: Black perspectives, by Rev. Jesse Jackson. p 12; Shirley A. Chisholm. p 13; Roy Wilkins. p 13.

New York Times. p 1. My. 6, '72. President bars birth curb plans. R. B. Semple, Jr.

New York Times. p 1. Ja. 23, '73. High court rules abortions legal the first three months. Warren Weaver, Jr.

*New York Times. p E 9. Mr. 7, '73. Each change has vast impact. Jack Rosenthal.

*New York Times. p 75. Ap. 9, '73. Population shifts upsetting the planning and use of suburban schools here. D. A. Andelman.

New York Times. p E 7. F. 17, '74. A surplus of space and teachers: in suburbs grown older, schools grow silent. Iver Peterson.

*New York Times Magazine. p 14-15+. S. 16; 11+. O. 7, '73. Should we pull up the gangplank? L. A. Westoff.

Newsweek. 77:78. Ja. 25, '71. Census sense: views of C. F. Taeuber and P. R. Ehrlich.

Newsweek. 77:80. F. 15, '71. Census surprises.

Newsweek. 77:37. My. 10, '71. Middle America; center of population.

Newsweek. 79:37. Ja. 3, '72. Social-security swingers: policy of Texas refinery corp.

Newsweek. 79:62. Mr. 13, '72. Why the poor are fewer.

Newsweek. 79:62. Je. 19, '72. Why the poor get children: findings of two major studies.

Newsweek. 79:75. Je. 19, '72. Falling birth rate. P. A. Samuelson.

*Newsweek. 80:86. Jl. 10, '72. Non-yankee, stay home!

Newsweek. 80:28. D. 25, '72. Baby bust: what the impact of a lower birth rate will be.

Newsweek. 81:27-8. F. 5, '73. Abortion revolution.

Parents' Magazine. 46:26. Je. '71. Population control: your child's future depends on it. Emerson Foote.

Parents' Magazine. 46:56. N. '71. Peril of overpopulation: our greatest threat. G. M. Landau.

*Parents' Magazine. 47:40-1+. Ap. '72. What do you want your children to learn about sex? E. W. Johnson.

Parents' Magazine. 47:64-5+. N. '72. New swing to small families. Winfield Best.

Physics Today. 26:9+. O. '73. Will zero-population growth hamper scientific creativity? [letter] A. J. Owens.

Public Opinion Quarterly. 35:93-9. Spring '71. Public attitudes toward population and pollution. R. J. Simon.

Reader's Digest. 101:131-5. N. '72. Our forgotten Americans. C. H. Percy.

*Reader's Digest. 103:135-9. Jl. '73. Surprises from the 1970 census. Trevor Armbrister.

Redbook. 136:12+. Mr. '71. How many children are we entitled to have? A. L. Goodstadt.

Religion in Life. 41:480-96. Winter '72. When fruitfulness and blessedness diverge. Beverly Harrison.

Saturday Evening Post. 244:8+. Fall '72. Population control. P. R. Ehrlich.

Saturday Review. 54:60. F. 6, '71. Who makes the babies? P. R. Ehrlich and J. P. Holdren.

Saturday Review. 54:56. Mr. 6, '71. Avoiding the problem. P. R. Ehrlich and J. P. Holdren.

Saturday Review. 54:4. Mr. 20, '71. Senior citizens lib movement. Goodman Ace.

Saturday Review. 54:61. My. 1, '71. Lost genius debate. P. R. Ehrlich and J. P. Holdren.

Saturday Review. 55:71. Ja. 1, '72. People in the machinery: views of Barry Commoner. P. R. Ehrlich and J. P. Holdren.

Saturday Review. 55:40-4+. Mr. 11, '72. Militant Malthusians: zero population growth movement. Wade Greene.

Saturday Review. 55:29-38. S. 23, '72. Double standard of aging. Susan Sontag.

Saturday Review of the Society. 1:30-5. Ap. '73. Abortion for the asking. Helen Dudar.

Science. 158:730-9. N. 10, '67. Population policy: will current programs succeed? excerpts from address, March 14, 1967. Kingsley Davis.

Science. 164:522-9. My. 2; 165:1203-4. S. 19, '69. Population policy for Americans: is the government being misled? Judith Blake.

Science. 170:132-6. O. 9, '70. Man and his environment; adaptation of address, March 19, 1970. A. J. Coale.

Science. 171:527. F. 12, '71. Nobody ever dies of overpopulation. Garrett Hardin.

Science. 171:1212-17. Mr. 26, '71. Impact of population growth. P. R. Ehrlich and J. P. Holdren.
  Discussion. Science. 173:278+. Jl. 23, '71.
Science. 172:1297. Je. 25, '71. Survival of nations and civilization. Garrett Hardin.
  Discussion. Science. 173:381. Jl. 30; 174:1077-8. D. 10, '71.
Science. 174:119-27. O. 8, '71. Toward the reduction of unwanted pregnancy; adaptation of address, January 21, 1971. F. S. Jaffe.
Science. 175:487-94. F. 4, '72. Ethics and population limitation. Daniel Callahan.
  Discussion. Science. 178:347-8+. O. 27, '72.
Science. 176:1085-90. Je. 9, '72. Population and pollution in the United States. R. G. Ridker.
Science. 177:1178. S. 29, '72. Population committee launched. C. Holden.
Science. 180:708-12. My. 18, '73. Teenage birth control dilemma and public opinion. Judith Blake.
Science. 180:1143-51. Je. 15, '73. Racial aspects of zero population growth. E. B. Attah.
Science Digest. 72:27-9. D. '72. Approaching zero hour.
Science News. 103:54. Ja. 27, '73. Abortion: court decision removes legal uncertainty.
Scientific American. 224:50. Ap. '71. Z.P.G.
Scientific American. 225:14, 17-25. Jl. '71. Census of 1970; with biographical sketch. P. M. Hauser.
Scientific American. 225:40. O. '71. Optimism and population: NAS report.
Scientific American. 228:46. F. '73. Leveling off.
Scientific American. 228:44-5. Mr. '73. Abortion decision.
Scientific American. 229:17-23. Jl. '73. Public policy on fertility control. F. S. Jaffe.
  Discussion. Scientific American. 229:8-9. N. '73. C. K. Levison.
Senior Scholastic. 102:12. Mr. 5, '73. 2020 vision.
Senior Scholastic. 102:17. Ap. 9, '73. U.S. birth rate sets record low.
Seventeen. 31:178. Je. '72. Americans must learn that continual growth is not the solution to all problems! Tom Dickman.
Social Education. v 36, no 4. Ap. '72. Special issue on population education.
Sociology and Social Research. 57:356-66. Ap. '73. Voluntarily childless wives: an exploratory study. J. E. Veevers.
Time. 100:43-4. O. 9, '72. Stopping at two.
Time. 101:50-1. F. 5, '73. Stunning approval for abortion: decision blow by blow.
Trans-Action. 9:55-66. N. '71. Hunger of old men. David Gutmann.

U.S. News & World Report. 70:25. F. 8, '71. Patterns of change in the United States; excerpts from address, January 25, 1971. G. H. Brown.

U.S. News & World Report. 70:62-4. F. 15, '71. Too many Americans? A population expert's view; excerpts from address, January 13, 1971. Conrad Taeuber.

U.S. News & World Report. 70:24-6. Mr. 1, '71. Where blacks are moving, and moving up.

U.S. News & World Report. 70:24-5. Mr. 15, '71. New profile of the U.S.; latest from census.

U.S. News & World Report. 71:56. N. 22, '71. Looking ahead to U.S. in year 2000.

U.S. News & World Report. 72:49. F. 28, '72. Fewer children for U.S. women.

U.S. News & World Report. 72:45-6. Mr. 20, '72. What the birth rate means to the America of year 2000.

U.S. News & World Report. 72:64. Mr. 27, '72. Ways to cut U.S. birth rate, findings of an official study.

U.S. News & World Report. 72:36-7. Ap. 10, '72. Where Americans will live in 1990.

U.S. News & World Report. 72:51-3. My. 29, '72. End of the baby boom: what it means to the country.

U.S. News & World Report. 73:59-62. D. 25, '72. Population slow-down—what it means to U.S.

U.S. News & World Report. 74:36. F. 5, '73. Supreme Court eases rules on abortion.

U.S. News & World Report. 75:72. O. 8, '73. End of rush to America's big cities? What has happened to the 50 top metropolitan areas.

Vital Speeches of the Day. 37:261-3. F. 15, '71. Patterns of change in the United States; address, January 25, 1971. G. H. Brown.

Vital Speeches of the Day. 38:697-703. S. 1, '72. Perspectives in the population crisis; address, June 15, 1972. S. P. Theisen.

Vital Speeches of the Day. 38:758-9. O. 1, '72. Population growth; address, August 22, 1972. W. L. Johnson.

*Washington Post. p 1. My. 6, '72. Nixon rejects population panel advice. H. F. Rosenthal.

*Washington Post. p 1. Ja. 23, '73. Supreme Court allows early-stage abortions. J. P. MacKenzie.

*Washington Post. p 1+. Je. 18, '73. D.C. population studied: age called a factor in crime. Lawrence Feinberg.

*Washington Post. p 18. Ja. 1, '74. Population hits 211 million.